Tanja Reiffenrath

From Ethnic to Transnational

masteRResearch

herausgegeben von / edited by

Walter Grünzweig, Randi Gunzenhäuser,
Sibylle Klemm, Sina A. Nitzsche, Julia Sattler

Band / Volume 8

LIT

Tanja Reiffenrath

From Ethnic to Transnational
Screening Indian American Families

LIT

Cover illustration: Dorothe Knapp

Bibliographic information published by the Deutsche Nationalbibliothek
The Deutsche Nationalbibliothek lists this publication in the Deutsche
Nationalbibliografie; detailed bibliographic data are available in the Internet at
http://dnb.d-nb.de.

ISBN 978-3-643-90584-0

A catalogue record for this book is available from the British Library

©LIT VERLAG GmbH & Co. KG Wien,   LIT VERLAG Dr. W. Hopf
Zweigniederlassung Zürich 2014   Berlin 2014
Klosbachstr. 107   Fresnostr. 2
CH-8032 Zürich   D-48159 Münster
Tel. +41 (0) 44-251 75 05   Tel. +49 (0) 2 51-62 03 20
Fax +41 (0) 44-251 75 06   Fax +49 (0) 2 51-23 19 72
E-Mail: zuerich@lit-verlag.ch   E-Mail: lit@lit-verlag.de
http://www.lit-verlag.ch   http://www.lit-verlag.de

Distribution:
In the UK: Global Book Marketing, e-mail: mo@centralbooks.com
In North America: International Specialized Book Services, e-mail: orders@isbs.com
In Germany: LIT Verlag Fresnostr. 2, D-48159 Münster
Tel. +49 (0) 2 51-620 32 22, Fax +49 (0) 2 51-922 60 99,
E-mail: vertrieb@lit-verlag.de

In Austria: Medienlogistik Pichler-ÖBZ, e-mail: mlo@medien-logistik.at
e-books are available at www.litwebshop.de

Contents

Introduction 1
1 Transnationalism and the Cinema 5
2 Transnational Relationships 15
3 Identity and (Trans)National Spaces 49
4 Happily Ever After? 67
Conclusion 95
Works Cited and Further Resources 101

List of Figures

2.1	Figure 1: *Mississippi Masala*, Mina at the supermarket	18
2.2	Figure 2: *Chutney Popcorn*, Reena and the dancers at the wedding	23
2.3	Figure 3: *The Namesake*, Ashima at the window	26
2.4	Figure 4: *Chutney Popcorn*, Reena and Lisa	32
2.5	Figure 5: *The Namesake*, Ashima tries on Ashoke's shoes	34
2.6	Figure 6: *Mississippi Masala*, Anil's and Chanda's wedding night	37
2.7	Figure 7: *Chutney Popcorn*, Mitch and Sarita in bed	44
2.8	Figure 8: *The Namesake*, Ashima and Ashoke in bed	47
3.1	Figure 9: *Mississippi Masala*, Mina in her room	55
3.2	Figure 10: *Chutney Popcorn*, Reena and Sarita at the vendor's booth	58
3.3	Figure 11: *The Namesake*, "Welcome to suburbia"	65
4.1	Figure 12: *Missippi Masala*, Mina's phone call	73
4.2	Figure 13: *Chutney Popcorn*, finding a place for Lisa in the ceremony	83
4.3	Figure 14: *Mississippi Masala*, ending	87
4.4	Figure 15: *Chutney Popcorn*, last shot	90
4.5	Figure 16: *The Namesake*, Ashima in India	92

INTRODUCTION

In 1916, when Randolph Bourne first uttered the term 'transnational,' he noted – with a pessimistic undertone – that the melting pot and the assimilation of immigrants, their 'Americanization,' had failed. Instead, he argued, the United States rather constitute a "federation of cultures," yet not a "distinctively American culture" (n.p.). Today, scholars have moved beyond notions of American exceptionalism and embraced the plethora of ethnic, cultural, social, economic, and political strands that link individuals and communities both on the national and global level. Consequently, the concept of assimilation of minorities to the dominant white Anglo-American culture is replaced by cultural transformations and pluralist identity constructions. In recent years, American Studies scholars have thus shown an increasing interest in the theoretical framework of transnationalism and even proclaimed the so-called 'transnational turn' in American Studies, a direction and directive that aims at responding to discourses of internationalization, (post)nationalism, and transculturation.

In an age in which telecommunication, cyberspace and globalized media produce connections beyond the boundaries of the nation-state, the cinema with its inherently transnational history lends itself to the critical analysis of the representations of communities which transcend national borders. Earlier studies have focused on racism and race-related issues, on intergenerational conflicts in immigrant communities, and the fashioning of relational identities in the Third Space, a space where new forms of cultural meaning may be produced, boundaries blurred, and established notions of identity and culture called into question (cf. Bhabha 103). Accordingly, the representation of homes, homelessness, and the return to one's home country have been regarded as central themes in diasporic literatures and films, in which nostalgia often loomed large. This book builds on the existing scholarship, yet focuses on the representation of the younger generation of immigrants and their controversial personal relationships which situate them in contact and conflict with their environment in the United States.

For this purpose, the films *Mississippi Masala* (1991), *Chutney Popcorn* (1999), and *The Namesake* (2006) will be analyzed. These films focus on the voices of members of previously marginalized communities and weave complex connections to various nation-states and ethnic groups, not least due to their production contexts: *Mississippi Masala*, directed by the New York-based Indian filmmaker Mira Nair, was shot in various locations throughout Mississippi and in Kampala, Uganda. Her film *The Namesake*, the adaptation of an eponymous novel published by the Indian American author Jhumpa Lahiri in 2003, too, takes viewers to settings on two continents and features scenes filmed in different West Bengali locations, among them Calcutta and Shantiniketan, as well as sequences produced in New York City, its northern suburb Yonkers, and Scarsdale in up-state New York. Considerably changing the focus of the novel, Nair has made Ashima, who is a housewife in the book and a singer in the film, a central character. Her role, especially her struggle in America, ultimately receives more attention in the adaptation. More than that, Nair has also moved the original setting of the novel from Cambridge to New York (cf. also Muir 234), a city conspicuously marked by immigration. In a similar vein, *Chutney Popcorn*, the film debut of the Canadian-born writer and director Nisha Ganatra, depicts inner city and suburban ethnic communities and was filmed on location in New York City. *Mississippi Masala* and *The Namesake* in particular achieved great popularity and a wide audience, while the independent film production *Chutney Popcorn* has been mostly recognized by the LGBT community. The selection of films therefore shows that the issues discussed can be found in both commercially successful and independent cinema.

Strikingly, all three films have endings that can be described as remarkably happy, if not utopian, considering the conflicts that have driven their plots. Almost too easily, the characters eventually find their places in their respective American and Indian communities straddling the divides of tradition and self-definition and mediating the demands of their families as well as their claims to agency. For film scholars Patricia Pisters and Wim Staat, families in the media are "both a symptom of and a remedy to cultural crisis" (12) and are thus assigned an ambiguous role in the push and pull of American values and the traditions that tie immigrants to their homelands. A cultural crisis is according to anthropologist David Bidney produced by difference separating people into conflicting groups and resulting in the suspension or disintegration of fundamental aspects of sociocultural life (536f.). Transnationalism then presents a challenge which may well be regarded as a cultural crisis that implicates anxieties and feelings of displacement as national boundaries cease to hold sway. Since neither traditions nor identities are fixed, but subject to constant negotiation, the fluidity of movements and definitions receives emphasis. Yet in how far are family structures that emerge in the midst of migratory movements or in multinational and multicultural communities symptomatic of the transnational condition and in how far may they remediate cultural crises?

Transnational cinema, as I will explain in more depth in Chapter 1, takes these issues as starting points and often interweaves different plot lines, quickly leading to conflict. In their beginnings, the films do indeed depict a cultural crisis caused by displacement, nostalgia, and rigid borders. However, toward the end of their plots, they create a seemingly positive world: crises are overcome and conflicts solved as soon as the characters become agents and actively engage in developments that will finally lead to a reconceptualization of the traditional family and established cultural values. I will therefore argue that transnational cinema becomes an instrument in the mediation of the cultural crisis presented by the changes of a transnational world. The films do not *per se* resist and depart from genre-specific conventions, core American values, and the traditions of the ethnic communities they depict. Instead, transnational cinema consciously employs established cultural practices, sometimes reinforcing, sometimes subverting them.

In the first chapter, I will establish the theoretical basis necessary for the analysis of the films. I will briefly outline the concept of transnationalism and highlight the aspects of transnational cinema that are crucial for my reading. In particular, this chapter will map the relations between 'transnationalism,' the national, and immigrants' identity constructions, contrasting it to older concepts employed in the analysis of culture, such as assimilation.

The second chapter will be devoted to the beginnings of the three films, since they contribute greatly to the interpretation of their endings. The beginnings draft the respective protagonists' relationships to their families and pose the question of how these familial ties reflect on the relationship between the protagonists' homelands and the United States, ethnic traditions and American values, and an understanding of family that privileges heterosexuality and biologically determined gender roles, as opposed to the reconceptualization of such traditional family structures. These potential sources of conflict reverberate in the wedding scenes that each of the films feature at their beginnings, as well as in the depiction of other love relationships. The second part of this chapter thus explores how the weddings portrayed here influence the overall plot of the films and their character constellations. Moreover, the role of the wedding in Hollywood cinema is studied and contrasted to its significance in the transnational films analyzed here to examine how the motif is transformed against the backdrop of a cultural crisis. Finally, this chapter will fathom the obstacles the lovers in the films face before a happy ending may conclude their journeys.

The third chapter will be concerned with ideas of space and differentiate two recurring settings in the films: the non-place, a transitory place epitomizing the transnational, and suburbia, a place associated with assimilation and the American Dream. Due to the films' engagement with migration, traveling, and border crossings, non-places, such as airports, motels, and streets constitute frequent settings. How do such non-places affect the protagonists' identity formations and what happens when characters attempt to settle permanently in the non-place, the first half of this chapter asks. The second half of this chapter will analyze the suburban setting and the devastating events taking place there which turn the suburban dream into a nightmare. Why might the films not end with the fulfillment of the American Dream?

The fourth and final chapter will offer a reading of the films' endings. Using Gilles Deleuze's and Rosi Braidotti's notion of 'nomadism,' the first part of this chapter probes the fact that it is not a protagonist's arrival that presents the end point of the plots, but that it is indeed their departure which concludes the films to ask how traveling and the protagonists' quest for identity are intertwined. The second part will consider the fashioning of a new family unit and analyze how these emerging ties affect the protagonists' location in their community. Finally, the last section of this chapter will provide a close reading of the final shots of the films, raising the question of whether they do indeed depict a lasting "happily ever after."

1 TRANSNATIONALISM AND THE CINEMA

"What would the field of American Studies look like if the transnational rather than the national were at its center?" American studies scholar Shelly Fisher Fishkin asks in her 2004 presidential address to the American Studies Association (21). Ethnic studies scholar Jigna Desai's definition of transnational cultural studies in turn may provide a preliminary answer:

> This new creature, transnational cultural studies, integrates the field of cultural studies, postcolonial and globalization studies, and black diasporic and Asian-American studies specifically in a way that challenges notions of culture as not being related to power relations, critiques of modernity and the nation, and political economy. In addition, this particular permutation also formulates the areas of feminist and queer studies as integral to this formation. (3)

While Desai clearly highlights the potential of transnational cultural studies to weave together a variety of disciplines in order to re-examine key categories, media studies scholar Andreas Jahn-Sudmann is quite critical of the term 'transnational' and quotes Leon Hunt and Leung Wing-Fai: "The word 'transnational' is used more often than it is defined, and definitions remain abstract by nature" (in Jahn-Sudmann 16).

In an attempt to clarify its meaning, media studies scholar Ricarda Strobel stresses that the term 'transnationalism' needs to be extended to also encompass 'transculturalism' and finds it crucial to include discourses of globalization, multiculturalism, interculturality and postcolonialism, whereas other critics explicitly distinguish between the concepts of 'transnational,' 'intercultural' and 'multicultural' (10f.). Although intercultural and multicultural issues are certainly present in the push and pull of transnational encounters, it is important to explicitly distinguish transnationalism from these earlier attempts to conceptualize cultural mediations in the discipline of American Studies. The 'transnational turn' of American Studies, Jahn-Sudmann then states, is not an attempt to mark trans- or interdisciplinary turns, but rather a turn within the discipline of American Studies (15). My objective in this section is thus to establish a definition of transnationalism on the basis of the existing scholarship. This chapter will show that the notion of 'transnationalism' calls for a critical rethinking of several established categories and concepts in cultural studies, such as 'nation,' 'assimilation,' and 'diaspora.'

Generally speaking, the term 'transnationalism' refers to the "economic, social and political linkages between people, places and institutions crossing nation-state borders and spanning the world" (Vertovec 1). Hence Fisher Fishkin argues that "over the past ten years a web of contact zones has increasingly superseded the nation as the basic unit of, and frame for, analysis" ("Crossroads" 21). On multiple levels, familial, religious, economic, social and political, immigrants are involved in their home and host societies – a feature that turns them into 'transmigrants.' Social relations link together their country of origin and their country of settlement and are crucial for any actions that are taken and decisions that are being made (Glick Schiller et al. xi).

Yet this does not mean that the nation as a category for analysis may be cast aside and substituted by global considerations only. Although (or rather because) the transnational easily crosses borders, its relationship to the national is quite complex. According to Elizabeth Ezra and Terry Rowden the transnational "at once transcends the national and presupposes it" (4). Thus an analysis of the transnational should not exclude the national. It is important not to misinterpret the transnational as an "anarchic free-for-all in which blissfully deracinated postnational subjects revel in ludically mystified spaces of ahistoricity" (ibid.). In contrast, Interpal Grewal argues that the strength of different nationalisms becomes visible within the transnational (35), an issue that the analyses in the following chapters underline since the films reveal that notions of race and heritage do remain prominent and that national ideologies and culturally marked gender roles crucially influence the conceptualization of transnational subjects. Jahn-Sudmann is therefore absolutely right in summarizing the transnational as covering any story that lies beyond the national, yet bears references to it (17). It is hence of particular interest to scholars to examine how hybridities and fluidities shape spaces that are territorially and culturally less stable than previously thought (Fisher Fishkin, "Crossroads" 21).

In this vein, the transnational is often seen in relation to the international, sometimes even used as a euphemism for the term 'globalization.' Many critics, on the other hand, purport that transnationalism not only applies to relationships between nations and societies, but also figures as an inside perspective into a nation (Jahn-Sudmann 16). In the essay "Theories of American Culture (and the Transnational Turn in American Studies)" Winfried Fluck's major concern is the function of transnational American Studies as an instrument to foster a better understanding of American culture. Reverting to Randolph Bourne's "Trans-National America" and his claim that the United States has no distinct culture, Fluck argues that this is in fact the case precisely because the country developed under special conditions (59f.), most prominently immigration. Earlier American Studies theorists felt the need to identify a "unique, specifically American identity" and "exceptional national virtues" in American culture, whereas Fluck considers it a "healthy antidote" to analyze the cross-cultural exchanges that have shaped it (61). In doing so, he encourages theorists to examine the possibility of resistance inside American culture (ibid. 65). The potential for resistance lies with multiple or hybrid identities for a simple reason: to focus solely on a particular group would mean to repeat essentialism; "there is no longer an outside of the system," Fluck notes. Furthermore, since all possible sources of resistance within American culture "have been used up," he urges critics to look beyond the borders of the nation-state (71f.).

Additionally, unlike earlier theoretical approaches, transnationalism does not treat cultural differences as separate entities, but places emphasis on the transformation of cultures through contact and interaction (Rowe 25). This means that cultural identity also becomes a product of negotiation and mediation. John Carlos Rowe demands that relevant theory does not limit cultural and social formations to processes of assimilation of "minor" cultures to a "dominant" culture (23f.) and Grewal, too, urges scholars to reconsider the concepts of 'assimilation' and 'acculturation' in order to provide a more adequate grasp on the experience of (im)migration:

> The production of state subjects, ethnic subjects, multicultural subjects, and transnational subjects were processes full of conflict and contradiction, as diasporas, nationalisms, 'global' feminisms, and multinational corporations – to name just a few of the key formations through which what is called 'global' is being understood in academic work as well as outside it – worked within and against the powerful narratives of the United States nation and state. (Grewal 9f.)

That the idea of assimilation is too limiting in a transnational context also becomes evident in the argument devised by American Studies scholar Emory Elliott. He points out that the majority of European immigrants strived for and eventually gained acceptance as "white Americans," as they adopted American values and taught their children English. Immigrants of color, on the other hand, had difficulties participating in the assimilation process. Consequently, many of them created their own communities and maintained a stronger attachment to their countries of origin (10). Whereas some immigrants may identify more with one society than another, anthropologist Steven Vertovec notes that the majority of immigrants maintain several identities linking them to more than one nation (6). Consequently, full identification with only one nation-state does not reflect the social reality of immigrants. In this respect it is fascinating to take a closer look at figures who have been marginalized due to the fact that they have crossed so many borders that they are "hard to categorize" (Fisher Fishkin, "Crossroads" 30), an approach that also points to the limitations of hybridity.

According to Vertovec, young people in particular select, mix or elaborate facets of culture and identity from several aspects of their heritage and transnationalism is thus frequently associated with constructed styles and everyday practices (7). For instance, in places outside India some basic Hindu rituals have been truncated or refashioned, while others have been "negotiated" in order to serve as socio-religious links between immigrants from different regions and traditions. Similarly, immigrants are also known to have "invented" a style or an entire corpus of rites (ibid. 142).

Furthermore, other theorists, among them media studies scholar Samir Dayal, call for a rethinking of the term 'diaspora' that goes beyond "the state-centrist model of allegiance to the host vs. the home country" (46). In his essay "Diaspora and Double Consciousness," Dayal discusses the importance of a double consciousness in transnationalism and stresses that it offers an interstitial perspective on what it means to be American. This perspective may then lead subjects to reconsider the notion of belonging and eventually arrive at a state in which double consciousness is not simply resolved, but "rather enables an internal critique while suspending the mundane question of assimilation" (47). In contrast to the common conception of double consciousness meaning "both/and," Dayal's approach may in fact be described as "neither this/nor just that." He attempts to see double consciousness negatively, thereby dissolving the positive constructions of diaspora that mirror the desire to belong to two or more cultures or places. This is necessary since nostalgia and credulity would otherwise prevent subjects from questioning existing narratives of race, class, gender, and sexuality (ibid.). Instead, he argues,

> [d]oubleness is more productively conceived as the interstitiality of entering (or leaving) and destabilizing the border zones of cultures, as fracturings of the subject that resist falsely comforting identifications and reifications. Its negative value is that it denies the subject's sovereignty and stresses the performativity of the subject. (48)

As a consequence, identity loses its stability and is instead turned into a relational and contingent process triggered by the ruptures of borders and the instability of cultural mediations.

Finally, as I have hinted at earlier, transnationalism has also had an impact on the definition of being American. Not only has the concept of Americanness been altered by location, place, and historical context, but also aspects such as race, gender, class, nationality, and religion are categories of major significance and thus aid in the formation of shifting and changing national subjects. Due to their ability to move across nations and national boundaries they produce American identities that are tightly intertwined with a global consumer citizenship (Grewal 8). Grewal sees Americanness as being transnationally constructed through cultural, political, and economic practices, so that "becoming American" does not always require full participation or belonging to a nation-state. Nevertheless the process of becoming American may indeed coincide with allegiances to other nationalisms or identities, often in conflictual ways. As identities are always in progress, becoming American should be seen as changeable, contingent, and historical (ibid.).

TRANSNATIONAL CINEMA

Film and cultural studies scholars Elizabeth Ezra and Terry Rowden point out that cinema has been transnational from its beginning as films often circulate freely across borders and use international personnel. This observation holds true for the era of Chaplin, Hitchcock and Fritz Lang and perhaps even more so for contemporary directors, among them Indian filmmaker

Mira Nair (2). While in the earlier stages of the history of film, transnationalism rather referred to means of production and global distribution, international marketing and merchandise, or post-processing techniques, such as dubbing to make films accessible to a wider transnational audience, these aspects have arguably moved into the background and are today frequently taken for granted.

For this study, I will therefore focus on the implications that transnationalism has for the content and the aesthetics of films. Jahn-Sudmann contends that film is particularly interesting for scholars since they find that the transnational experiences they observe and analyze are treated increasingly self-reflectively by filmmakers (23). Of course his argument is likewise valid for literature, yet it should not be dismissed, since film may offer a heightened degree of self-reflexivity as it employs not only language, but also visual material and sound. In this context it should be noted that personal experiences of ethnic minorities are not only a topic in the independent film genre, but have also entered popular and commercially successful forms of Western cinema where these films have entertaining, and often didactic value. Cinema thus plays a significant role when it comes to the analysis of transnational relationships in the United States.

However, the question of transnational film as a separate genre is to some extent contested, an issue that is certainly rooted in the fact that the term delineates an academic category rather than an established genre that may be marketed to target audiences. In the introduction to the volume *Film Transnational und Transkulturell* Ricarda Strobel even remains undecided whether a new genre has been founded or whether these films simply constitute another chapter in international film history, and whether they may ultimately redefine popular cinema (13). Other critics are more explicit and pronounce transnational cinema as an umbrella term for the plethora of films of various genres and approaches to filmmaking dealing with global mobility.

Hamid Naficy's concept of 'accented cinema' is one of these approaches and constitutes an aesthetic concept grounded in experiences of displacement, especially due to exile and diaspora. Unlike other scholarly perspectives, Naficy's concept places a strong focus on the filmmakers, as he argues that similarities of the films merely lie in "what the filmmakers have in common" ("Situating" 111). In this study I use the term 'transnational cinema,' since I would like to distance myself from an auteur-centered model. Additionally, Jahn-Sudmann notes that 'transnational cinema' *de facto* represents something that may immediately be connected to transnationality (22). He contends that with the proclamation of a transnational cinema as a new genre cutting "across previously defined geographic, national, cultural, cinematic, and meta-cinematic boundaries" filmmakers have the possibilities of reflecting critical and novel ideas in international media (20). I will thus attempt to outline the genre of transnational cinema.

First of all, despite the fact that the notion of genre is an inherent part of scholarly engagement with films, critics hardly agree on a common definition (Buscombe 11), yet most see genre formation as connected to society. Not only does each period create its own narratives and genres, but the stories told have an impact on the perception of the age, as well as the culture. What then, is a genre? Film scholar Andrew Tudor begins his definition of genre by illustrating that the films grouped in one genre share certain features (3): They might narrate similar stories and typical actions, involve similar characters, or use common setting or props (cf. also Buscombe 14f., Tudor 4). When such patterns are repeated in a number of films, they may constitute the corpus of the genre. Genre hence depends, as Buscombe aptly phrases it, "on a combination of novelty and familiarity," since audiences enjoy watching a film when they recognize conventions they know, expect, and understand, yet also encounter generic elements that are innovatively altered (21). Genres are therefore not inalterable systems, but instead reflect a "regularized variety" (Naficy 205f.). In other words, the films I have chosen do not follow one possible plot or depict only one character constellation; hence a one-to-one comparison will not provide deep insights. However, there are strong recurring themes, motifs, and aesthetic devices in the films which the directors treat quite differently as they engage with the genre, utilize it to play with the viewers' responses (Tudor 8), or comment on the genre or other films.

According to Naficy, transnational films belong to a genre of narratives and cine-writing that is subject to certain generic and thematic conventions. To an equal extent, they are also products of the filmmakers' transnational location in time, place, social life and cultural difference. These linkages allow for films to be read and reread "not only as individual texts [...] but also as sites for intertextual, cross-cultural, and translational struggles over meanings and identities" ("Phobic" 204f.). Furthermore, transnational cinema is not restricted to a certain genre, but may integrate various types of film (ibid. 205). The films that I will discuss here belong to different genres or are hybrids and include elements of the romance, comedy and drama, for the narratives of transnational cinema may be told in a variety of different genres. It is hence not the genre which makes a film transnational, but its narrative, themes, motifs, and of course its subjects. Obviously, major themes include migration and diaspora.

For Naficy, significant components of the transnational film constitute narratives or iconographies of memory, desire, loss, longing, and nostalgia. He describes memories as "fallible, playful [and] evasive;" thus the narratives and iconographies that are produced by memories may be fragmented or constitute embellishments or elisions ("Phobic" 205). Therefore the plot often does not evolve in a linear fashion, but is interrupted by flashbacks or consists of a sequence of scenes revealing leaps in time and space. The narrative is often initiated by the loss of the characters' home and receives its dynamic through their attempts to find a new home. Physical movement across borders is then of course intertwined with emotional and psychological conflict.

In this context, Ezra and Rowden speak of the characters as "people caught in the cracks of globalization" (7), a phrase that highlights an initial sense of loss and disorientation much better than the notion of the cosmopolite that Ezra and Rowden also consider in their definition of the genre. They aptly note that the concept of the latter is problematic in so far as it is broadened and made more complicated when displaced people fashion a space for themselves and their "experiences of transnational consciousness and mobility," arguing that the search for a new home makes the immigrant a cosmopolite, but at the same time subverts the potential for cosmopolitan identification (ibid.). I will return to this question when I introduce Rosi Braidotti's notion of the nomad, a subject who essentially transcends boundaries.

While I strongly agree with Ezra's and Rowden's idea of a reconceptualization of the naturalized and normative notion of 'home,' I have to disagree with the argument made in their introduction to *Transnational Cinema*, namely that the outcome of transnationality is loneliness which manifests itself in "desolate structures of feeling" and lonely characters

(7). On the contrary, the transnational condition involves productive processes of restructuring relations, particularly with regard to questions of home, identity, and familial ties. In *Negotiating Identities: An Introduction to Asian American Women's Writing*, Helena Grice for example notes that Asian American women are preoccupied with problems of space, place, and "home." These issues serve as metaphors for the dynamics of identity: "The slippage from 'Who am I?' to 'What's my place in the world?' is seen in many texts by Asian American women" (199). Needless to say, departures, wanderings and homecomings play a crucial role. Grice points out that the house is the "most powerful psychospatial image" and is interchangeable with the idea of 'home.' 'Home,' of course, is more than a dwelling place – it is connected to belonging, origins and nurturance (ibid. 200). Interestingly, the house has an important function in representations of immigration as well as in American cultural life: the sense of belonging involves ownership, i.e. claiming territory or owning a house. Due to its history, American cultural production has included carving out and claiming territory; Grice states that American self-definition includes the definition of space. Therefore one may say that immigrant texts reiterate the importance of the house (ibid. 203). Just as transnational American Studies may serve as an instrument to overcome American essentialism, transnational cinema can establish a "minority" cinema that grasps various points-of-view and gives a voice to minorities and their conceptions of cultural and social identity and acknowledges their struggle for cultural spaces.

Finally, another aspect of transnational cinema that is quite crucial is its location in culture. It is located between the global and the local in the in-between spaces of culture, thus criticizing ideas of cultural purity and separatism (Ezra and Rowden 4). Likewise the settings of the films to be analyzed constitute in-between spaces, areas that are linguistically, culturally, and nationally fragmented (Rowe 24). *The Namesake* and *Chutney Popcorn* are set in New York, a city that more than any other city in the United States has been shaped by its immigrant population. *Mississippi Masala* on the other hand is mostly set in Greenwood, Mississippi, a city in which Indians, Blacks and whites live separated from each other, yet frequently cross into each others' spaces. Furthermore so-called 'non-places' are significant when talking about identity formation in transnational film:

characters spend a great amount of time in hotels, airports or on the road, and it is in these spaces that they develop some of their most important relationships (Ezra and Rowden 8).

2 Transnational Relationships

The beginnings of the films introduce the protagonists' family and love relationships and, directly linked to these, the emerging conflicts that drive the plots. This chapter will discuss the initial scenes in which viewers encounter the protagonists and their personal struggles, as well as the first scenes depicting newly developing love relationships, as these scenes set the tone of the films and also vividly demonstrate the significance of familial ties for immigrants in the transnational world.

In their introduction to *Shooting the Family*, Pisters and Staat note shifts in the definition of the bourgeois nuclear family as well as the extended tribal family and pose the question whether contemporary movements of migration and the ubiquity of audiovisual representations of the family may be held responsible for these transfigurations, since in the transnational world, the family is regarded as both the mediator and the mediated as traditional values are negotiated:

On the one hand, we claim that the family is under pressure and being altered by the forces of globalization and migration. On the other hand, family matters of all kinds, pertaining both to the reinforcements and radical reconfigurations of traditional family values, are increasingly constructed and refigured in a mediated form: the 'reel family' has become an important medium for intercultural affairs. (7)

In the films under analysis the family plays a crucial role in the immigrants' identity formation. On the most basic level, the family embodies traditional values of the culture of origin, in this case the Indian culture (ibid. 19). It also represents the family members' ties to the homeland, often expressed through references to family members who have been left behind. Nevertheless, as Pisters and Staat argue, home is no longer automatically connected to the families' homeland; as a result, the family is torn between the place where they live (home) and the place where they were born or where they have their origins (homeland) (10) and likewise the family values in the target culture and the culture of origin are often seen as conflicting. However, the concepts of family, home and homeland are tightly intertwined, for not only does the family offer a sense of belonging and stability, but older family members also reinforce traditions. Consequently, a triadic relationship is established in which the family stands between home and homeland, mediating the influences of each. Generally speaking, families may then serve to affirm the immigrants' identity or influence their identity formation.

The films highlight the resulting conflicts as the protagonists become aware of the fact that traditional family ties put constraints on their identity, their location in American society and their self-definition as women, ethnic individuals, as well as sexual subjects. The characters then either deconstruct the heteronormative, nuclear family in order to construct a support system that responds better to their needs or leave their family altogether, turning into nomads in Braidotti's meaning of the term.

For Pisters and Staat, these mediated families are "both a symptom of and a remedy to cultural crisis" (12). In my introduction, I have already elaborated on issues that may well constitute a cultural crisis in the transnational world, among them subjects that have been displaced through exile or migration and need to recover their home and construct their identity. However, I disagree with Pisters and Staat when they state that the "expression of the desire for stability projects the family as the answer to a cultural crisis caused by the contradictions of globalization" (ibid.). On the contrary, the films evince that the "answer" is rather presented by a strong sense of individualism and the departure from prescribed paths and the problem certainly lies in the notion of stability. Although a desire for stability in the sense of consistency and fixity may well be understandable in an ever-changing environment, it is ultimately associated with rigidity and a resistance to movement and change. Longing for stability would hence imply closing oneself off from the living conditions in a transnational world, an issue that would finally increase the feeling of displacement and result in an even greater conflict. Although they do yearn for stability and permanence, the characters in the films are compelled to rework the notion of stability and thereby actively engage in the constant flow of cross-national exchange. Film scholar Sonja de Leeuw is right when she holds that "dealing with discontinuity involves a search for continuity that allows for the construction of a new 'home'" (43), yet home is no longer a fixed and stable place and continuity may also be grasped as continuous movement and ongoing traveling.

Displaced and "Out of Place"

All three films depict protagonists who have been displaced, yet their situation is more complex than migration from one country to another may initially suggest. In this vein, transnational cinema features characters that are not only displaced, but also "out of place" because they possess the motivation for constant change. These characters, my readings will show, are highly dissatisfied with their current situation, a situation that provokes conflict, and strive for change, eventually resolving the conflict.

In *Mississippi Masala*, Jay's family have already faced their expulsion and the end of their prosperous life in a Uganda oppressed by Dictator Idi Amin in 1972. During the opening credits, a maps traces the family's journey from Uganda to Great Britain and then to the United States before the plot continues – eighteen years later – in Greenwood, Mississippi, a town with Indian, African-American and white American population. In Mississippi, literature and film scholar Binita Mehta maintains, the family is twice displaced: first of all as "Indians by culture" and secondly as "Ugandan by birth" (156), which is an observation that holds especially true for Jay's daughter Mina, since she is not only displaced like the rest of her family, but strikingly "out of place" in their new home.

Usually the immigrants' families offer acceptance and support in a new environment. However, this is not the case here: Jay's family is not fully accepted by their relatives because of their low economic standing and therefore denied any possibility for stability in the first place. Whereas Kinnu, Jay's wife, nonetheless attempts to create stability and earn the relatives' recognition by running her own business and finding a suitable Indian husband for her daughter, Jay continues to devote all his time and efforts to suing the Ugandan government for his passport and property, trying to restore the stability the family once had in Africa. Mina's behavior, on the other hand, differs from that of her parents since she reacts actively to her exclusion and increases the distance to her family.

Mina is also the first character the viewer encounters in the Mississippi setting. At the Piggly Wiggly supermarket, she and her aunt buy milk for her cousin's upcoming traditional Indian wedding. The Piggly Wiggly is in fact a well-established Southeastern chain of supermarkets which claims to be "America's first true self-service grocery store," a business idea that revolutionized shopping in America and provided customers with more conveniences and services (Piggly Wiggly n.p.). The store thus represents a distinct American space: The big shelves are neatly stacked with bottles, cans, and boxes and in most shelves every space is filled, representing choice and abundance.

Here, not only Mina's appearance provokes stares, but also the shopping cart full of buttermilk cartons and milk containers she is pushing (see figure 1). The cartons and containers are piled up in a disorderly fashion in her cart and hence present a sharp contrast to the mise-en-scène of the supermarket which is dominated by straight and parallel lines connoting stability and a sense of strict order. Mina scurries in order to get out of the supermarket quickly, and briefly disappears behind a large pyramid of red Coca Cola cans. Symbolizing not only the American way of life, but also the American economy, the soda cans underline the supermarket's importance as a strongly marked American space, emblematic of the American setting in which Mina and her family now find themselves.

Figure 1: Mississippi Masala, *Mina at the supermarket*

On their way to the checkout, viewers become aware of the conflicts within the family for the first time when her aunt asks her if they should buy toilet paper because it is on sale, an allusion to the Indian relatives' material interests that constitutes a recurring motif throughout the entire film reproducing the popular stereotype of the Indian American. Unlike her relatives, Mina has no such interests; instead, she responds with a lack of comprehension and impatience: "Aren't we late? I thought you wanted milk for the wedding." It is striking that the first sentences she utters in the new setting express her unwillingness to interact constructively with her aunt. More than that, she and her aunt do not even speak the same language, for while she addresses Mina in Hindu, Mina responds in English. Mina's communicative behavior – she hardly makes eye contact, either – implies great distance between her and her aunt. Neither of them is willing to switch languages to accommodate the other and communication is not negotiable.

The scene at the supermarket is therefore significant for the understanding of Mina's character in relation to the transnational. The setting seems too distinctly marked as American to serve as a ground for transnational encounters, although all the three ethnicities that define Greenwood's demographics in the film are present, as not only Mina and her Indian aunt are shown at the Piggly Wiggly, but also an African-American employee and a white American cashier. Rather, it is a space in which American and Indian cultures remain static and appear at polarized ends. It becomes clear that Mina, who has never been to India, refuses to speak Hindi, and also lacks understanding and patience for the culture her aunt embodies. On the other hand, she cannot assimilate to the American culture either, since her appearance as well as her habits mark her as the "other" who is not accepted by the white American characters at the supermarket. Hence she neither aligns herself with her aunt nor with the white cashier who, on seeing the amount of milk the two women wish to purchase, jokingly remarks: "Holy cow, are you opening a dairy?" and promptly meets Mina's angry gaze. However, there is also a brief moment foreshadowing the solidarity between Mina and other people of color, since the Black employee, too, shakes his head at his white colleague's statement. Yet panethnicization, i.e. the ways in which different, previously unconnected ethnic groups forge a sense of belonging (cf. Lien, Conway and Wong 22), Asian American studies scholar Susan Koshy contends, is rather a product of social processes than cultural bonds

(334). All in all this sequence illustrates that Mina's behavior does not express acts of assimilation, but at once responds to and also heightens her sense of displacement. Koshy further notes that in a transnational reading, ethnicity may not be understood in terms of whether and how American culture incorporates Asian Americans; instead, ethnicity has to be deterritorialized (322f.).

Moreover, the relationship between Mina and her aunt lacks the intimacy of relatives living together, which the subsequent scene in the car elucidates. While Mina sits in the driver's seat, her aunt has chosen to sit in the back seat, a constellation that first of all highlights the physical and emotional distance between them. It can be read as Mina turning her back on her aunt but also as her aunt distancing herself from Mina, taking the comfortable and superior position of someone who lets others drive them. The latter reading is reinforced by a camera shot panning along the car depicting the aunt counting dollar bills while the Black supermarket employee loads their groceries into the trunk. The shot indicates a line of causality with the Indian woman's economic well-being resulting from business with white Americans and service from African-Americans, which corresponds to the social hierarchy amongst whites, Indians, and Blacks that the film constructs. Mina, the only character in this sequence who changes places when she moves around the car, literally and figuratively moves between these different groups, transgressing the rigid hierarchy. The shot therefore symbolizes the relationships between the ethnic groups in the film and in the course of the plot, Mina is a character who crosses into other spaces whereas her family try to keep themselves separated from the rest of the Greenwood population and adhere to racial purity and the self-inscribed laws of color hierarchy.

Early on in the film it becomes obvious that Mina feels much more connected to African-American than to Indian culture. When her Indian date Harry Patel takes her out to a club in the Black part of Greenwood, she immediately feels comfortable among the dancers and is known and respected there. However, her character cannot be grasped in terms of fixed categories of ethnicity and nationality, another reason why a setting that denies cultural cross-over and negotiation makes her appear uncomfortable, restless and maybe more rebellious than it would seem appropriate for a woman in her twenties. As a consequence, she will eventually have to leave Greenwood and her Indian relatives.

Another perspective on displacement is offered by the film *Chutney Popcorn*. Set in New York City, the film tells the story of two Indian American sisters, Reena and Sarita, who were apparently born there and are fully integrated into their respective communities despite the fact that they lead very different lives. Whereas Sarita is engaged to Mitch, a white American, Reena is in a relationship with a young American woman named Lisa. Comparative studies scholar Jaspal Singh characterizes Reena as "headstrong" and "independent," a reason why she continuously struggles with her mother's ideal of a "good Indian girl" (164). As a consequence, diasporic displacement is not visible at first sight but becomes evident when first- and second-generation immigrants interact. Especially Reena's sexuality is a constant source of conflict and marks her as an outsider in the Indian community who clearly prefers the heterosexual relationship model.

It is noteworthy though that Reena's and Lisa's relationship is introduced before the depiction of the heterosexual marriage and postcolonial studies scholar Anupama Arora is certainly right when she maintains that this editing choice effectively works to subvert the status of heterosexuality as natural and the "'original,' that which comes first" (33). In this vein, the entire film celebrates the normality and everyday lives of various homosexual couples. However, Reena conspicuously falls out of the "norm" once she is amongst her mother and other Indian relatives, for her mother strongly adheres to heteronormative family structures and is careful to hide her daughter's sexuality from other members of the Indian community and their extended family.

Reena's uneasy relationship with the Indian culture and her Indian family becomes evident in the initial scenes after the opening credits. The first shot focuses on a yellow gift with a red ribbon attached to the back of Reena's motorcycle. To the viewer's surprise Reena attends her sister's wedding reception as a guest and is not involved in the ceremony and the rituals that observe Indian heritage and traditions as well as constitute Sarita's and Mitch's heterosexual union. Likewise, the reception only represents a brief visit into her mother's and sister's culture. As the camera pans along the moving motorcycle, the viewer sees Reena in the traditional

Indian sari – combined with her black leather jacket, heavy boots and helmet. These different clothes signify both her Indian and her lesbian identity (Arora 33). Yet obviously Reena is neither comfortable nor used to wearing traditional Indian clothing: the head wind blows the long fabric into her face and she struggles to get it out of her way. Later on she confides to Lisa that she feels like she is "in drag."

Worse yet, they arrive at the reception only in time to wave the newlyweds off, a situation that establishes Reena's role as the "black sheep" in her family. As her Indian relatives stand on the sidewalk, waving after the couple in their car, Reena rushes past them, still in her leather jacket and with her helmet on. "Worry about mum," her sister replies when Reena apologizes for being late and a short sequence of point-of-view shots between Reena and her mother, Meenu, follow: The first shot shows a medium close-up of Reena, who has turned to look at her mother, followed by a shot of her mother standing in front of a crowd of Indian women, looking reproachfully at her daughter and folding her arms, thus distancing herself. The power of her stare is multiplied since the other women gaze angrily at her, too. The sequence is briefly interrupted by a shot of Lisa next to the bike taking off her helmet, as Meenu notices that her daughter has brought her girlfriend, and then goes back to Reena, whose eyes now seem sad. While she is standing still, the sari fabric from her shoulder glides down, an effect that is emphasized by a clinging sound and literally underlines the falling mood. The sound also ends the soft synthesizer music that has accompanied the lesbian couple's motorcycle ride since the opening credits and during the point-of-view shots, some lower tones intermix, hinting at the brief moment of disappointment and conflict between mother and daughter. The two only exchange gazes in this sequence and do not talk to each other which suggests that conflicts are either silenced or occur on a regular basis so that words are not necessary anymore.

Reena's role as an outsider in the Indian community becomes even more obvious as the wedding celebration in the backyard goes on. One of the Indian women tells her to join the others on the dance floor, saying "you, too, have Punjabi blood," whereupon Reena turns to her mother and asks her if they actually are Punjabi. "You know absolutely nothing," her mother angrily replies and her accusation reveals Reena's lack of knowledge about her own heritage and culture, yet also exposes her mother as a character who is constantly dissatisfied with her daughter's behavior. Throughout the film there are several brief moments of intimacy between mother and daughter, but they quickly pass and are always superseded by her mother's demands or criticism, as the followings shots, too, indicate: While some of the guests start dancing, Reena and Meenu stand aside with plates of food in their hands. In this scene Meenu appears to be mothering, but also patronizing as she takes some food and puts it into Reena's mouth. Interestingly, in another scene, when Lisa's mother visits the young women at their home, she brings Reena a bag of food. These instances give the impression that Reena is considered somewhat helpless, unable to take proper care of herself. Besides, Reena's mother remarks that all she wants are grandchildren and paradoxically asks Reena: "are you too selfish to give me that?" "Mum, I'm lesbian, not sterile," Reena replies and her mother urges her to be quiet in front of the other relatives, since, after all, she has introduced Lisa as "Reena's roommate from college."

Figure 2: Chutney Popcorn, *Reena and the dancers at the wedding*

Another sequence that is crucial for the introduction of Reena's character as an outsider is a scene in which all of the wedding guests are dancing and she stands in front of the crowd (on the right hand side of the screen shot), her back turned to the camera (see figure 2). Whereas the traditional clothes accentuate the female bodies of the girls and women who are dancing and moving their hips, Reena seems rather clumsy in her dress. The guests are cheerful and the slow motion of the scene highlights the protruding movements of their arms and their jumping back and forth as they dance. Reena, in contrast, does not move at all. After a few seconds, though, she turns and walks away with her eyes looking down. Although her movement is captured in slow motion as well, it seems to be at a different pace than the movement of the dancers. The fact that she and the group are not in proportion to one another – Reena is in the foreground, yet not far away from the others and therefore she appears unnaturally big – creates the impression that they are moving on separate levels, in separate cultural spheres.

Finally the diegetic Indian music coming from a speaker on the other side of the dance floor is drowned out by "Pretty Song," a slow rock song by the all-girl band Frogpond. The first lines of the lyrics, "missed my chance to chance my way/I know it happens every day" capture Reena's disappointment and only trail off when she is back in her own home in the next scene. The superimposition of Punjabi and English music hence marks a dissonance, "a push and pull," between Reena's Indian and her lesbian versions of self that result in an "uneasy in-between existence" (Arora 37).

In *The Namesake*, the viewer is first introduced to the young protagonist Ashima. After her marriage is arranged, Ashima moves to New York with her new husband Ashoke and their initial encounter and quick wedding mark the beginning of the family saga that covers more than twenty years. During the final parts of the opening credits, Ashima is introduced to the viewer as a young student of classical Indian music. Sitting in a bright courtyard, she sings to the instrumental accompaniment, her facial expression and gestures in tune with her song. A long shot depicts her occupying the center, whereas the other students are sitting on the right, facing and following her. This shot illustrates that Ashima not only immerses herself in Indian traditional practices, but is also fully integrated into her life in India.

When she arrives at home after her lesson, her mother informs her that Ashoke and his parents are already waiting to meet her. It is during this short conversation that the relationship is agreed on and Ashima's future is decided: since Ashoke is pursuing a Ph.D. in New York, the couple will live in the United States. "My child, have you ever flown on a plane?" Ashoke's father asks her. "Will you be able to go halfway around the world? Live in a cold city with freezing winters?" Then he switches dramatically to Hindi: "Leave your house, far from your parents?" The dialogue elucidates that language is an important tool to convey meaning and identity. Especially at the beginning of the film, the characters choose to speak Hindi to address familial concerns and intimate matters, while English is the language associated with leaving one's home and beginning a new life.

After their traditional Hindu wedding ceremony, an establishing shot locates the scene in New York and announces the couple's arrival in the United States. There it is winter and the neighborhood is covered with snow. The lack of colors contrasts sharply with the rich colors of the previous wedding scene, thus creating an atmosphere of desolation. It is quiet when Ashima wakes up; only the sound of the passing train and the drops from icicles can be heard from outside, adding to the feeling of loneliness, strangeness, and sadness. Slowly Ashima rises and her first look is directed to the other side of the bed where she assumed her husband to be lying. Ashoke, however, is gone and only hesitantly, she moves through the apartment looking for him. In his analysis of *The Namesake*, Himadri Lahiri states that "change of geographical location is the first shock" (3), an assertion that is underlined by the fact that Ashima feels physically unwell in their new apartment due to the New York winter that makes her freeze in her thin Indian dress, rendering the traditional item of clothing out of place in the new geographical space.

Ashima's discomfort is furthermore highlighted when a medium close-up shows her leaning against the door frame in front of an almost empty apartment. On the one hand, her posture indicates that she is in need of stability and support, while at the same time, her position limits the space she takes up to a minimum and bespeaks a desire to disappear from the bleak scene. Although white wallpaper with patterns covers the walls in the apartment, the room behind her appears utterly dark. Together with her downcast and closed eyes, the shot conveys sadness and disappointment. Clearly, Ashima is not yet at home in their new home and, as Lahiri maintains, comes to experience "the intensity of the loss of the family and community support" (3).

Moreover, the literal frost of the season also suggests a figurative cold, because a second, more significant state of uneasiness – both for Ashima and the viewer – is constituted by her lack of rapport with her new husband Ashoke. When he finally enters with a bag of groceries, he does not greet her, but instead plainly notes: "It is freezing today outside." Without taking further notice of her, he then turns to unpack the groceries while mumbling to himself, which emphasizes the couple's frosty relationship. When Ashoke mentions that they will buy the rest of the groceries when he returns from work, she is surprised: "You're going out?" "Yes, I must go. Three weeks are up," he replies and it becomes evident that whereas Ashoke is firmly integrated into a life in New York, Ashima remains behind, not knowing what to do. Another medium close-up looks past her through the window of the apartment at Ashoke who is now leaving and the focus moves from him to her as she raises her hand, causing the outside to blur (figure 3):

Figure 3: The Namesake, *Ashima at the window*

This shot is emblematic for Ashima's dislocation in her new home for several reasons. First of all, it denies her agency, since the camera is looking past her, for her, instead of with her in a point-of-view shot. Secondly, it depicts Ashima confined behind the window: she can look at the world outside, yet is denied participation. In addition, this scene is accompanied by the same melody that Ashima sang to at the beginning of the film, a melody that establishes a longing for home. However, this time Ashima's voice is missing; she has become silent and a fundamental aspect of her identity has disappeared. Her being "out of place" is therefore not only physical, but also psychological.

Comparing the films, one finds that traveling to the United States often results in dislocation, in some cases nostalgia for the homeland India. Generally, though, the films are concerned with a variety of feelings of estrangement in addition to the estrangement from home itself. By placing a strong focus on the immigrants' relationships to their families or partners, the beginnings foreshadow great conflicts with regard to questions of belonging and staying in a certain place. Furthermore, the initial scenes reveal the protagonists' agency, or often rather lack thereof in the face of displacement. Finally, these shots also insinuate the conflict potential inherent in the family structures themselves which illustrates that from the start, the families' original stability, too, is put to the test or has already begun to diminish, leaving the families indeed under pressure.

WEDDINGS RECONSIDERED

As I have noted above, another plot element all three films share in their beginnings is the celebration of a wedding. When analyzing these wedding scenes it is crucial to situate the films in the context of their respective genres. Weddings, of course, figure prominently in the romantic comedy, the genre that has shaped Hollywood cinema from its beginnings and indeed continues to form one of its major cornerstones (Grindon 1). Yet romantic comedies may just as well be encountered in transnational films produced outside the Hollywood industry, such as *Mississippi Masala*. Frequently, the genre is dismissed on account of its formulaic plot lines and, as David Shumway so fittingly phrases it, romance has "come to be almost a synonym for illusion" (381). Nevertheless, the films of this genre do lend themselves to a critical reading, because according to film scholar Leger Grindon, they portray conflicts that are central to the human experience and expose conventions surrounding social issues, such as generational conflicts, gender relations, and sexuality (1). These issues are treated lightheartedly and veiled in humor as a means to both make fun of the events and protect the characters from harm. As a consequence, the audience is provided with cues for a positive outcome and expects the film to end happily, commonly in the marital union of the two protagonists (ibid. 2). Marriage therefore becomes the goal of the lovers' pursuits and Shumway is absolutely right in assigning ideological force to the idea of romance and especially marriage, arguing that the films affirm marriage "in the face of [...] a growing divorce rate" yet do not trigger the audience's engagement with this aspect, for marriage is "mystified" (381, 384), most obviously by the fact that romantic comedies typically do not depict the couple's life beyond the wedding day.

Beyond their fundamental role in romantic comedies, weddings may of course also give rise to or conclude the conflicts triggered in dramatic films and hence assume a significant role in the drama genre as well, a genre concerned with the protagonists' struggles in everyday life. Film scholar Constantine Santas assigns an important role to drama as the "most prominent form of artistic expression" and outlines the genre's key themes, such as alienation, failure, death, crime, gender and racial issues, and the effects of globalization (31). With its wide range of topics, 'drama' serves as an umbrella term for number of different subgenres rendering the survival of traumatic events and the overcoming of loss ("Drama" 1). Nair's *The Namesake* is a transnational drama, focusing explicitly on themes of alienation and exclusion, problematizing generational conflicts, particular with regard to Indian traditions and the disintegration of familial structures as Ashoke dies and Ashima laments the apparent Americanization of their children. Finally, *Chutney Popcorn* is a hybrid of both genres, featuring dramatic as well as comedic elements.

Since all three films depict weddings only in their beginnings, they do not follow the so-called 'marriage plot' in order to arrive at a happy ending and weddings and the depiction of marriage serve a different function in these films. They reflect the characters' attitudes towards tradition, as well as develop new familial structures and ties. "The power of [the] traditional family ideal lies in its dual function as an ideological construction and as a fundamental principle of social organization," sociologist Patricia Hill Collins states and adds that families constitute "primary sites of belonging" (157). Besides, weddings are important since they offer a space for "celebrating cultural traditions, continuity and community" (Arora 33). Arranged marriage, however, highly conflicts with romantic love, as my further analysis will show. Furthermore, the films reveal that, once marriage is used to merely fulfill traditions, it causes deep discontent in the characters.

In *Mississippi Masala*, Mina's family and their relatives celebrate the traditional Indian wedding of her cousin Anil and his wife Chanda at the relatives' motel where they live. However, at the wedding reception, only a few brief shots actually depict the groom and bride and the camera work privileges the depiction of the guests who engage in the celebration, which gives the impression that the reception is not so much a celebration of the love-relationship the newly-weds lead than a symbolic ceremony praising the institution of marriage and celebrating Indianness. An establishing shot shows the Monte Christo's luminous advertising in the dark, locating the wedding scene at the motel, one of the most significant settings in the film that I will discuss in more detail in the next chapter. Diegetic Indian music leads into the scene and the camera focuses on Kinnu, who is kneeling on a small stage, singing, while two men at her left and right are playing the tabla (Indian drums) and a harmonium. Behind her there are two chairs that are upholstered with the same red cushion that will later in the film reappear on the couple's bed in the scene depicting their wedding night and the recurring fabrics and patterns elucidate the standardization of the motel rooms. Although the room in which the reception takes place is decorated with drapery hanging from the ceiling and the walls, it lacks individualizing details. As the father Jay and Mina are making their way through the rows of guests, the moving shadows of a ceiling fan are visible and add to the rather Spartan atmosphere of the room in contrast to the solemn occasion. Furthermore, all the windows in the room are closed with curtains or blinds, reflecting the group's isolation.

The wedding ceremony illustrates the significance of Indian traditions and rituals for the extended family and their members' identities. A number of shots focus on Kinnu singing, reinforcing her role as the family member who values Indian traditions and customs, practices them, and proudly flaunts them. Anil's father then invites the guests to join him in a prayer song, reminding them: "[E]ven though we are 10,000 miles away from India we should not forget our roots, our culture, our tradition and our gods." As the guests start singing, it quickly becomes apparent that not all of them share the same appreciation of traditions and the knowledge about them: The guests are comically out of tune, only a few of them clap rhythmically and rather hesitantly, some mumble and others seem to move their lips quietly. Consequently, the Indian community at the reception lacks a shared understanding about what constitutes tradition and how these traditions are to be practiced. Nonetheless the scene illustrates that most of them do adhere to the idea that they need to hold on to Indian traditions.

As the camera pans along the rows of guests, several shots are noteworthy and of particular significance here, because they indicate that the family is unsettled in their celebration of Indian traditions and that the adherence to rituals only superficially ties them together and cannot provide a lasting sense of stability. Four older women dressed in white are shown sitting at the side of the room in front of a mirror, watching the other guests. The camera in turn watches them watching, while it also catches a glimpse of the mirror in which their image is reproduced. The mirror and its reflective quality are indeed of importance during the performance of the prayer and the entire reception, since the camera keeps showing characters gazing into the mirror, watching themselves as if checking on their behavior. The mirror then serves as an instrument of affirmation within the community. A comical element is added to the portrayal of the four women, when one of them is filmed fanning herself with a small battery-driven fan. Needless to say, the noise produced by the fan can be heard through the prayer song and although it does not interrupt the ritual, it is quite distracting and further illustrates that the traditional prayer rather functions as a superficial, but institutionalized ritual than a practice meaningful for all participants.

On the one hand, one may assert that it is modernity, signified by the fan, which disrupts the unity of the extended family in their celebration. More importantly, though, their disunity also has its roots in their migration paths and the family members' affiliation with Indian culture. Mina, for example, does not join the prayer either, but nods her head to the rhythm of the song. Having been born in Uganda and having never travelled to India, Mina cannot relate to the song and for her, the ritual therefore has at best entertainment qualities. Mehta states that for the older generation, the practice of rituals may indeed help them to maintain a sense of identity. For the younger generation, however, rituals are often meaningless, as this scene underlines (164).

While *Mississippi Masala* relates the wedding of two Indians, *Chutney Popcorn* renders scenes from the bi-cultural wedding of Reena's sister Sarita and her white husband Mitch. The problem in *Chutney Popcorn* is certainly not arranged marriage or a lack of love in marriage, since the first shot of the wedding celebration depicts Sarita in her Indian wedding dress, smiling, before the camera moves to Mitch, who is sitting next to her. The couple sits in front of a number of guests, but their faces are outside the frame so that only Sarita's and Mitch's faces are visible, a shot that places the couple at the center of their ceremony. Yet at the same time, Sarita's mother demands: "You promise to have many children, ok? Not just one or two. Three, four . . . as many as God blesses you with, alright?" Hence their wedding is important because it marks the beginning of a family unit that is supposed to do justice to Indian conventions and the demands of others, which the film aptly problematizes in its course when it becomes evident that Sarita is unable to conceive a child.

Collins outlines the imagined traditional family ideal as follows: "[f]ormed through a combination of marital and blood ties, ideal families consist of heterosexual couples that produce their own biological children" (156). Similarly, the beginning of the plot reveals that it is Sarita's and Mitch's greatest wish to have children. The wedding sets high expectations in motion and having children is presented as an obligation, not as a choice. Sarita is imagined as the carrier of tradition that provides cultural continuity through biological reproduction (cf. also Arora 35). After the wedding she therefore proudly announces to Reena that she and her husband are now trying to have a baby. "It's so predictable," Reena shakes her head while Sarita is angry and replies "What? It's something we've never done before!" Later, Reena and Lisa joke among themselves that Sarita is fulfilling all of her mother's dreams.

On the one hand Sarita's and Mitch's wedding puts into practice both expectations and traditions. On the other hand, Arora holds that the very notion of marriage is denaturalized when Lisa and Reena emerge as a couple through rituals much like Sarita and Mitch (33). Central to their bonding is mehndi, the application of henna, a ritual that in South Asia is a practice performed by and for women, often as a part of the wedding ritual (ibid. 32). During the opening credits, several close-ups depict Reena's dark hand applying henna to white female bodies. A medium shot then shows Reena and Lisa in bed (see figure 4).

Figure 4: Chutney Popcorn, *Reena and Lisa*

Reena is holding her and carefully renews a faded henna tattoo around Lisa's arm. "If I had a real tattoo I wouldn't have an excuse for you to be touching me all the time," Lisa smiles and their physical closeness and the intimate exchange of looks leave no doubt that the two are a couple.

Another close-up shows Reena's hand as she wrings out a piece of wet cloth in front of a white background in order to wash the paint off and thereby complete the tattoo. This shot alludes to the universal and ceremonial quality of the ritual and mehndi is thus disconnected from its original meaning, while Arora would even go so far as reading the scene as a mockery of the heterosexual Indian wedding ritual (33). As the plot proceeds, the impression is confirmed that mehndi is a ritual of what Arora has termed the "queer diaspora," constituting erotic practice as well as exotic good, when Reena not only applies it to her partner Lisa's body, but also to the skins of other young women who enter the beauty parlor where she works. It is then by means of henna that Reena fashions her "chosen lesbian family" (ibid. 35).

Like *Mississippi Masala*, *The Namesake* depicts an arranged marriage between two Indian spouses, albeit one that takes place in India. Yet in contrast to the other films, *The Namesake* does not portray the wedding of minor characters, but it is that of the protagonists whose relationship is initiated by their parents. Therefore, arranged marriage does not merely function as a counter perspective to the "chosen" romantic relationship in this film, but is central as the only form of relationship. Whereas especially *Mississippi Masala* mocks and heavily criticizes traditional Hindu marriage, *The Namesake* offers a more sympathetic approach. By focusing on the character of Ashima from the beginning, the film counteracts the charge of "women as commodity" (Kaplan 176). Since both the conversation between the parents and their children and the actual wedding ceremony take place in India, their home country is established as a place connected to tradition and the order of familial structures and ties.

The decision that Ashima will accompany Ashoke to the U.S. therefore receives great significance. While her mother's voice can be heard in a voice-over, praising Ashima's talents in front of Ashoke and his parents, Ashima's gaze falls on Ashoke's shoes in the hallway and the camera pauses on the new elegant brown and white leather shoes imprinted with "Made in the U.S.A." Right then, non-diegetic music (another classical Indian song) sets in and marks her noticing of the shoes as a significant moment. After a careful glance in the direction of her parents, Ashima lifts her sari und slips her feet into the shoes, smiling proudly. She takes a few steps, with her eyes fixed on the shoes that are of course too big for her, and then turns towards the camera, as if posing in front of a mirror (figure 5).

The shot depicts her in the middle of an otherwise empty hallway, hinting at the strong sense of isolation that Ashima will initially experience when she follows her husband to the United States. In a similar vein, the

Figure 5: The Namesake, *Ashima tries on Ashoke's shoes*

clash between the Western shoes and the colorful Indian sari signifies the clash of cultures her emigration will trigger. Against the backdrop of a vast and magnificent hallway in which the colors have faded and the paint has begun to crumble away from the walls, the shoes may also be read as a sign of the material comfort that she hopes awaits the couple in the U.S. More than that, however, the scene shows Ashima literally walking in Ashoke's shoes, possibly connoting a desire to understand him, to really be with him. All in all, one may well argue that in this brief scene, Ashima silently chooses her husband, which is important for the quality of their relationship and the viewer's sympathetic understanding of their marriage. Years later, when the couple talks about their relationship, Ashima states: "I liked your shoes," a statement which confirms this reading.

The depiction of their Hindu wedding ceremony follows right after the conversation between the parents and is surprisingly brief. However, several aspects should be noted: First of all, the viewer gains the impression that Ashoke is highly uncomfortable in his role as the groom. When he is surrounded by women who try to cover his eyes before his bride enters, he seems awkward. Apparently, he is not familiar with the ritual, as he struggles to free himself of their hands. This idea surfaces repeatedly in the film, because Ashoke often relies on "the American way" whereas Ashima questions beliefs and contrasts them to her Indian ideals. Like in *Missis-*

sippi Masala, traditions are reinforced by the mother. Secondly, the wedding scene is accompanied by laughter, giggles, and happy screams which create an atmosphere of joy. Additionally, an old woman turns to Ashima during the ceremony to tell her: "You're starting a new life. [...] It's a new life full of happiness and joy." Therefore the wedding as such receives a positive connotation in this film. Nevertheless, the film problematizes the aspect of arranged marriage in so far as it becomes obvious that the newly-weds hardly know each other and even during the ceremony, their eyes meet only for a split second. The fact that they still are strangers to each other is something I will examine closely in the next section.

ROMANCE AND SEXUALITY

In romantic films, "love invariably strikes where it is forbidden," sociologists James Dowd and Nicole Pallotta correctly observe (552). The films in this genre then depict a form of romance in a conflictual context because it means (1) social ostracism, or at least disapproval by society or (2) the presence of a serious obstacle. Both *Mississippi Masala* and *Chutney Popcorn* present conflicts that arise because of the characters' choices of partners. In *The Namesake*, the conflict is more subtle and takes place in the private sphere of the newly-weds' home, resulting from the fact that their marriage was not an act of love, but of tradition. This section will therefore analyze the protagonists' love relationships and pay special attention to the scenes that depict physical intimacy, because these depictions are symptomatic of their relationships.

The scene depicting Anil's and Chanda's wedding night in *Mississippi Masala* is especially interesting when looked at in the context of the preceding and subsequent scene. In the preceding scene Demetrius, a young African-American, has given Mina a ride home from the club. While his van is parked in front of the motel, they say goodbye and Mina reveals that she is still single, suggesting her interest in him. As she leaves the van on the passenger side, closes the door and walks towards the entrance of the motel on the left, a point-of-view shot from Demetrius's perspective inside the van shows her walking in front of a sign announcing "Anil weds Chanda" and an arrow pointing to the left. This establishes a connection between their flirt in the van and the ongoing wedding night. However, the sign already hints at the contrast between the two relationships. The impression that Mina is attracted to Demetrius is reinforced as she looks back at him, smiles warmly, and waves. The sign, on the other hand, has the character of a makeshift wedding announcement because it is not festive at all, but rather plain like any other offer that the motel would announce on the side of the road. In line with its makeshift character, two light bulbs appear to be broken. Anil's and Chanda's wedding likewise receives the status of something plain that needs to be shown to the public but is actually worn out and lacks passion and love. While Mina follows the arrow pointing to the left and enters the motel, her Indian home space, the last shot of the scene shows Demetrius backing out and driving away in the opposite direction. The end of this sequence thus suggests that the lovers' worlds are in opposition to each other and foreshadows that if Mina follows Demetrius, she will have to turn away from the Indian home.

The subsequent scene then further problematizes Anil's and Chanda's arranged marriage. Depicting their wedding night, the entire scene is dominated by the color red. In Indian tradition, red is not only the color of bridal dresses, but is also associated with sexuality in marriage relationships as it alludes to heat and fertility. So, on the surface level, the couple has adhered to Indian wedding traditions, however, any form of romance, heat or physical intimacy is absent from the scene: While Chanda is asleep in her wedding dress, Anil wears blue pajamas and leans against the bed-head. He is restless, his feet twitching, and undetermined how to react to the situation. Moreover, there is no music in this scene, as viewers familiar with the conventions of Hollywood cinema would expect, that would turn the bedroom into a romantic setting. On the contrary, the only sound that can be heard is the buzzing noise of a fly, which is not only annoying but also mockingly destroys the prospect of romantic atmosphere.

This mockery of the conventional wedding night continues when Anil decides to take the initiative, turns to face his sleeping wife. As he gently touches her hair, the viewer may still have expected Chanda to open her eyes and gaze lovingly at her husband. However, she simply mistakes his touch for the fly, slaps him and continues sleeping (see figure 6). The entire scene therefore mocks their traditional relationship from a Western perspective by showing that although it may adhere to traditions, it does not contain any visible sign of love or physical contact and therefore does

Figure 6: Mississippi Masala, *Anil's and Chanda's wedding night*

not fully qualify as a relationship in Western eyes. I agree with philosopher Thomas Wartenberg who maintains that *Mississippi Masala* satirizes the institution of arranged marriage (156). His observation that archaic or ethnically inflected practices can only lead to either revolt or discontent (160) may well describe the situation depicted in this scene but does by no means apply to all ethnic traditions and customary practices the characters in the film are involved in.

The next scene between Chanda and Anil is framed by two intertwined scenes depicting the developing love relationship between Mina and Demetrius so that the Indian married couple serves as a double of the Indian and Black protagonists who are head over heels in love. Whereas the latter have already kissed for the first time, the relationship between the newly-weds has not changed. As the wedding reception is the viewer's first encounter with Chanda and Anil as a couple, their relationship is not only perceived as publicly and culturally accepted, but also as self-evident. Compared to the secret relationship Mina and Demetrius lead, it appears to be static and based solely on the interest to publicly uphold the traditional ideal of marriage, since, once again, there is no exchange of love or affection between them.

This impression is underlined by the fact that the scene is filmed from a high angle with the camera looking down at the couple. Strikingly there are no point-of-view shots or other changes in perspective that would add personal views to the scene. Like the scene of their wedding night, this scene is also set in Chanda's and Anil's bedroom and shows both of them lying on the bed. Although they have now switched places, with Anil lying on the right side and Chanda on the left, their situation has not changed. This time, however, Chanda is not sleeping, but only seems to have her eyes closed, as her facial expression is tense and she reacts quickly to Anil's touch. Her behavior thus shows open rejection and an attempt to separate physically from Anil, an act that is emphasized by her body language, for her arms are bent away from Anil and also her head is slightly turned to the other side.

Their problematic relationship is also reflected in a small framed photo of him and his wife on their wedding day that viewers notice on Anil's nightstand. The photo is both an attempt to preserve the memory of their wedding and a proof that it actually did take place – considering that otherwise the two do not resemble a married couple. Strikingly, even the photo lacks physical closeness: Anil appears to have his arms behind his back, whereas Chanda is slightly turned away from him. Moreover, their difference in size in the photo is emblematic of their unequal status as partners, for while Anil also appears individually in other scenes, Chanda only seems to have a meaningful role as his wife.

Parallels in the aesthetics of this scene and the scene of their wedding night serve to intensify the couples' emotional distance. Like in the scene of their wedding night, there is no music to create a romantic or intimate atmosphere and there is only silence between them. However, the color red is predominant in this scene as well, repeating the allusion to heat and sexuality. There is even a red light shining from somewhere so that also the couple's skin and the white bed linen appear slightly red. Nevertheless, the attempt to connect marriage and sexuality in a meaningful and comfortable way fails and Anil is obviously frustrated when he first takes a look at his own body under the sheets, then looks at Chanda, back at himself and decides to take action. The sequence of his looks first of all exposes Chanda as an object that is meant to fulfill his sexual needs. In stark opposition to a loving sexual relationship, she is appalled when he rolls over to lie on top of her, opens her eyes and asks him: "What are you doing? It's paining." After pushing him off of her, she turns so that her back faces Anil and closes her eyes again. The position of the couple is now almost the same as in the beginning of the scene, underlining the static nature of their relationship, yet they have established even greater physical distance between themselves.

More than that, the two newly-weds seem to be able to block out each other's presence entirely when Anil takes down headphones from the bedpost and switches on the television. The blue light emerging from the television drowns the red light, thus breaking off the topic of romance and sexuality. The theme of unfulfilled dreams and desires, however, continues on screen where a man claims: "I'd like to help everybody in America. I'd like to help the average person who is sitting at home, sitting in this audience. You all have dreams but you're maybe afraid to go for those dreams." The discontent that Wartenberg has addressed earlier is in this case publicly acknowledged. Mehta adds that whereas the film portrays the sexual frustrations of Anil and Chanda, it depicts Mina's and Demetrius's sexual relationship as "so intense and fulfilling that it empowers them to abandon family ties." She argues that given Mina's restrictive background and the repression of female sexuality in Indian society, her sexual relationship is liberating (163).

Moreover, *Mississippi Masala*'s portrayal of the two lovers and the representation of their relationship and the conflicts it causes firmly situate the plot in the context of the conventional romantic comedy. In this study on *The Hollywood Romantic Comedy*, Grindon describes the traditional plot as one initiated by unfulfilled desire as one or both lovers suffer from disappointment (9). Mina is, as the first section of this chapter has illustrated, "out of place" in the company of her extended family and her relationship with her parents is seriously affected by this as well. Later, the viewer learns that Demetrius, too, is unhappy because his relationship to Alicia, a local celebrity, has failed. The romance is initiated in the romantic comedy when the two lovers meet for the first time and, to use Grindon's words, "sparks fly" (ibid.). When Mina and Demetrius meet for the first time after she has driven her aunt's car into his van, he does not seem particularly interested, yet on their second meeting, when they dance together at the club, a series of point-of-view shots indicates his interest, even though viewers are right in presuming that his initial interest is motivated by the desire to make Alicia jealous. Afterwards, first dates follow (cf. Grindon ibid.) and Demetrius asks Mina to visit him at home when the family celebrates his grandfather's birthday. Later on this day, the two take a walk along the riverbank, where they kiss for the first time.

It is then, Grindon notes, that the prospective relationship of the couple is conventionally prohibited by the central conflict, introduced by a parallel plot line (ibid.). In Nair's film, two parallel plot lines work to spoil the lovers' attraction to each other: first of all, Jay's ongoing lawsuit against the Ugandan government, and his subtle racism directed at Blacks, and, secondly, Demetrius's occupation as a carpet cleaner providing services to the Indian family's motel. In the romantic comedy, the lovers will then try to circumvent these obstacles by leaving their usual surroundings (Grindon 10) and in this vein, Demetrius and Mina secretly spend two days at the Biloxi beach, where they also sleep with each other for the first time in a scene I will analyze in greater detail below. Midway through the film, the conflicts increase when Mina's relatives discover the relationship and accuse Mina of disgracing the family. As she and Demetrius become the talk of the town, Demetrius loses his clients, is on the verge of losing his business and thus, in line with the conventional plot, forced to make a decision. To rescue his carpet-cleaning business, Demetrius is determined to leave Mina and sue her family for the car accident. Simultaneously, Mina's relatives urge the family to leave the motel because they have caused trouble and continue to be a financial burden. When Jay decides that the family will then relocate back to Uganda, Mina runs away in order to find Demetrius.

In the final scenes of the romantic comedy, Grindon identifies a moment of epiphany and the resolution that reunites the couple (ibid.). I will analyze this sequence in the final chapter. In this context, it is, however, important that romantic comedies conventionally end in marriage or at least the prospect of marriage and rarely depict a family life beyond the wedding day. The three films, however, feature weddings only in their beginnings and hence develop a critical perspective on marriage. While *Mississippi Masala* contrasts traditional marriage and romantic love, *Chutney Popcorn* further attempts to substitute the normative marriage relationship by alternative support systems. *The Namesake*, on the other hand, takes a more sympathetic stand on traditional marriage, yet explores the conflicts arising from arranged marriage and the ensuing displacement at length. All films ultimately convey a message that favors romantic love and in this fashion very much adhere to the conventions of Hollywood cinema.

The scene that follows the rendering of Anil's and Chanda's static and disappointing marriage in *Mississippi Masala* is a sex scene between Mina and Demetrius. Constituted by several close-ups of the entangled bodies stressing the intimate atmosphere, it presents a sharp contrast to the preceding shots of the Indian newly-weds. There is African music in the background and Mina's heavy breathing underlines the sensuality and passion depicted in the scene. Even though in the morning their love is judged as the ultimate act of betrayal and shame both of them could bring on their families, the depiction of their sexual encounter carries only positive connotations.

"Demetrius, wish me a happy birthday," Mina demands after they have slept with each other. Some critics, among them women's studies scholar Susan Stanford Friedman, read this scene in Freudian terms. She argues that Mina's love for Demetrius triggers memories of Okelo, Jay's best friend in Uganda, and interprets Mina's memories of Uganda and Okelo as a longing for her father that emerges when the Black Demetrius sings "Happy Birthday" to her (30). Undoubtedly, the subtext of betrayal lingers in Nair's film and opens up the possibility that Mina may in fact be Okelo's and not Jay's daughter, for instance when Okelo and Kinnu hold each other for a long time when the family says goodbye to Okelo in Uganda, or when Mina comments on the fact that her skin is darker than that of her parents by referring to herself as a "darkie." Nevertheless, the memory of her birthday that follows is important for another reason, since it is then that her family watches Idi Amin accuse the Indians in Uganda of adhering to their principles of racial purity. Obviously Mina has just broken this ideal and thus one may read the scene as the celebration of the "birth" of Mina's character as a constant border-crosser.

Once their relationship is discovered by Mina's relatives in the morning, sanctions on legal, cultural and familial levels follow: Demetrius and Mina are arrested after a fight with her relatives, ostracized by their respective ethnic communities and are not allowed to see each other anymore. Consequently the non-functioning, but culturally encouraged and celebrated relationship stands in harsh opposition to the secret and scorned, but sexually fulfilling connection. At this point of the plot, a happy ending for Mina and Demetrius is not in sight. Stanford Friedman rightly remarks: "Like all utopian moments, [the scene] leaves us with a lingering question about how long it can last in the 'real' world of racial separateness, stratification, miscommunication, and silence" (30). The following scenes develop powerful depictions of conflict based on cultural and historical difference (ibid. 31) and I fully agree with Mehta when she purports that Mina has broken the social taboos of her own community, as well as of society at large, an act that she calls "revolutionary [...] for an Indian woman under any circumstances" (162).

Chutney Popcorn moves back and forth between the homo- and heterosexual couples and while the editing privileges neither orientation, it still disrupts heterosexuality as the normative way of life (Arora 33). It is probably the visibility of the lesbian relationship that strikes viewers and Indian characters alike, for Collins states that by foregrounding heterosexuality as the traditional family ideal, lesbian sexualities usually remain invisible (159). Queering then provides a critique of the normative (Desai 30).

Ideas about sexuality are also shaped by the norms held by the older generations and the entire ethnic community and are thus connected to questions of belonging. According to Desai, "heteronormativity operates as a crucial sign of belonging in diasporas" (30). Jaspal Singh argues that the fact that Reena's mother does not name her daughter's sexuality does not mean a denial of her lesbianism, but she simply does not "see the need for it" in the sense that "many first generation immigrants do not see the need to name their children's sexuality" (167) and, beyond that, naming Reena's sexuality would make her American (166). Although it is true that Meenu does not want to name Reena's lesbianism (she talks about it in terms of a disability or silences her), Singh's argument lacks precision with respect to the film: Meenu after all does deny her daughter's lesbianism, or at least her seriousness about her partnership with Lisa, e.g. when she arranges a meeting with her cousin who is supposed to take her out on a date or when she demands that Reena find a man. Furthermore, this concept of identity construction is much too simplistic here and once again collapses into ideas of assimilation and an "either/or"-approach to the fashioning of the self. Nevertheless it should not be neglected that questions of sexuality tie in with questions of Indianness. Holding on to traditional ideals of Indianness in transnational spaces becomes "doubly oppressive" for women due to racist and sexist elements (Singh 140). *Chutney Popcorn* therefore elucidates that ideas of Indian womanhood are no longer considered a given and instead aims to present new ideas and forms of Indianness, contesting and reconstructing traditional notions (ibid. 136).

In the previous section I have emphasized the importance of having children for Sarita and Mitch. When they find out that Sarita cannot become pregnant, the couple is devastated and Sarita even apologizes to her husband. Needless to say, her reaction is bitter when the doctor tells the sisters that Reena is healthy and could become pregnant if she wanted to. Reena's offer to act as a surrogate mother puts a strain on both relationships, as several scenes illuminate. One scene depicts Sarita and Mitch together in bed and is framed by two scenes that show the lesbian lovers in their attempt to fertilize Reena. The non-diegetic music is the same in these scenes and thus links them tightly to one another, allowing for a contrastive reading of the two couples. While Sarita has been criticizing her sister's and Lisa's probable lack of hygiene and precision, Mitch, on the other hand, replies that "all the energy" between the two lesbian lovers can only be good for the baby, thereby attaching a greater sexual connotation to the lesbian relationship than to his own.

This impression is reinforced by a shot of him simply climbing over his wife in the bed, while her gaze follows him. In the next shot, the camera films the edge of Sarita's and Mitch's bed from a lower perspective, so that only their feet and legs in pajama pants are visible (figure 7). The geometric shot with the horizontal line of the bed and the vertical lines of the curtains connotes the order, fixity, and rigidity of their relationship. Moreover, the inclined lines of the curtain behind Sarita underline the force with which she pushes Mitch off when he tries to get closer to her, running his leg over hers. In this encounter, Sarita is clearly disgusted by the thought of her husband thinking about her sister and the fact that familial and sexual boundaries cease to have clear cuts makes romance between the lovers impossible. The camera work, too, reflects this by depicting only the couple's feet in this scene, i.e. the least popular body part in Indian culture because it is associated with dirt. Sarita later confronts Mitch in the bedroom by saying "I feel that this situation is having an adverse effect on our relationship." Point-of-view shots between the couple follow, but whereas Mitch sees Sarita from a closer perspective, she sees him from a greater distance,

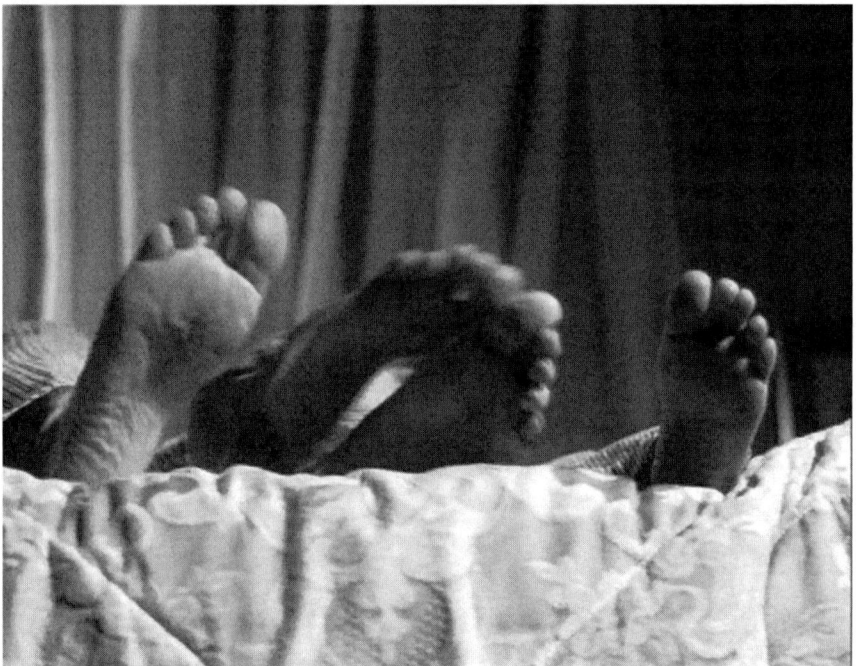

Figure 7: Chutney Popcorn, *Mitch and Sarita in bed*

which implies has distanced herself from him, which is underlined by her formal and rehearsed statement.

When she finally tells Reena to quit trying to become pregnant, she has come to the conclusion that she has been attempting to have a child "for everyone else" and realizes that all her attempts to fulfill others' social and cultural expectations have made her utterly unhappy. "It never occurred to me that I couldn't have children," Sarita states and on other occasions, too, she refers to becoming parents as something that is more imposed on them by an outside force or by fate, instead of something that she and her partner can actively choose. According to Grewal, the process of embracing modernity and choice is a vexed process for most characters that is only successful when disengaging from the "homogenized culture" that adheres to traditions (64). Reena, who has embraced choice in terms of both sexuality and motherhood, is therefore presented as an outsider to the Indian culture.

Likewise Sarita feels threatened in her role as a cultural authority when she offers to drive Reena's motorcycle, thereby switching roles with her sister:

> Mitch: "Honey, you driving a motorcycle is about as likely as . Shiva having a penis."
> Sarita: "That makes no sense."
> Mitch: "Yes it does. Think about it."
> Sarita: "Shiva is a man."
> Mitch: "No, he's not. All Indian gods are genderless."

Without looking at her husband she walks past him and angrily picks up the telephone in order to call her mother, the ultimate cultural authority in the film, to confirm her standpoint. As she ends the conversation, she turns to Mitch: "I don't need Reena showing me how to be a woman and I don't need you teaching me how to be Indian." Arora argues that only later does Sarita begin to realize that motherhood is a choice for her, too, and not choosing it does not mean negating womanhood (35). In this scene, though, she sees the signposts of both her female and Indian identity threatened.

The Namesake shows the thriving relationship between Ashima and Ashoke after they arrive in New York. While their conversations at the beginning do not develop beyond basic necessities of life, such as grocery shopping and how to turn on the hot water, their relationship becomes more intimate as their distance decreases. After Ashima has accidentally shrunk her husband's clothes at the laundromat, she goes into another room and closes the door to hide her tears. Ashoke's attempt to make her smile after he has apologized for being angry and persuaded her to open the door constitutes the first intimate conversation the two lead. They are still separated by the door frame that figures as a thick vertical border in the shot, but have become physically and emotionally closer.

An establishing shot that shows their neighborhood still covered in snow distinguishes this scene from a scene in which their relationship clearly has progressed. Now, the chirping of a bird elucidates that some time has passed and the cold is fading. This is underlined by the fact that the couple has ceased to wear heavy clothes and gloves inside the house; like the snow outside, the physical and emotional coldness between them is beginning to fade. Ashoke is lying on the floor, a cigarette in his right hand and he explains the subway map to his wife, who is sitting next to him. Their relaxed postures illustrate that they are comfortable with each other. "What if I get lost?" Ashima asks and raises her eyebrows, as if teasing him. Their eyes meet and he replies: "Why are you scared? Will I get you lost?" Ashima then grins and turns her head away. This gesture is the first instance in the film that may be understood in terms of a couple falling in love.

The next shot from above shows the couple in bed. The camera perspective underlines that there is still distance between Ashima and Ashoke, yet their relationship is growing: They are lying on their sides, facing each other. Their bodies are separated, but their knees touch and also their heads are close to each other, indicating that the two are forming a unity. Ashoke then takes his wife's hand and places it in the space between their bodies. Her right hand is still painted with the traditional Indian wedding symbols and reminds the viewer of their marriage. The camera follows his initially clumsy hand in close-ups while it moves along parts of Ashima's arm, across her shoulders, and removes her sari. The physical contact is obviously initiated by Ashoke, but a close-up of Ashima's right foot gently running down her left leg alludes to potential pleasure and indulgence on her part. However, as Ashoke's hand moves under her clothes, her face shows pain and fear rather than pleasure. After they kiss, the camera assumes a position from above again, distancing the viewer from a scene that is by no means violent, but uncomfortable to watch. Their bodies are intertwined, their hands tightly holding on to the body of the other. Strikingly, both of them are still wearing their clothes, emphasizing the inhibition and lack of intimacy that still divides them (see figure 8).

A quick cut ends their physical encounter and shows a train rushing past loudly, an image that recalls traumatic memories in Ashoke and makes him rise from his sleep. This scene is significant because it introduces the motherly aspect of Ashima. "Come close to me," she says in Hindi and takes her husband's head in her arm, holds him gently and starts singing to him. Tellingly, Ashima finds her song back at this instance: in this scene, a significant aspect of her identity is given back to her, but ultimately connected with another that will become increasingly important as the plot proceeds, namely her role as a mother. Her figurative role changes into the actual

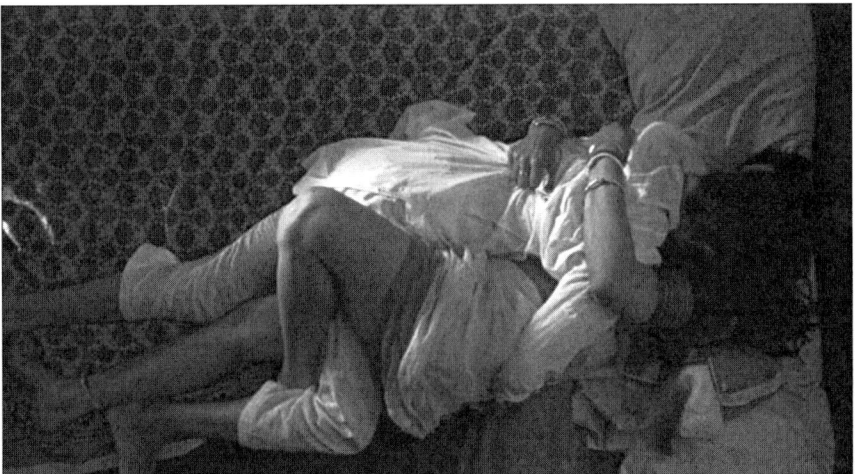

Figure 8: The Namesake, *Ashima and Ashoke in bed*

role in the next scene, in which she is already pregnant and at the hospital. Consequently, their physical contact is directly connected to Ashima's pregnancy and hence pleasure is subordinate to procreation, as Lahiri also notes that pregnancy will lead to family formation (3). Sexuality and romantic love in this film are therefore only displayed as means to an end.

All in all, sexuality and romance are treated quite differently in the films. In *Mississippi Masala*, the fulfilling physical relationship between Mina and Demetrius serves to mock the relationship of her relatives and likewise the depiction of Anil's and Chanda's marriage also works to expose the shortcomings of a traditional arranged Indian marriage. In *Chutney Popcorn*, homosexual romantic love serves to deconstruct normativity and calls into question the given roles of women. In the scenes showing the heterosexual couple Sarita and Mitch, the lack of romance and the strained relationship between the two demonstrates Sarita's frustrations over failing to fulfill cultural expectations. Like in Ganatra's film, *The Namesake*, too, links sexuality to the founding of a family and romantic love only enters Ashima's and Ashoke's relationship after the wedding. Despite these differences, in all films sexuality and romantic love serve to distance the protagonists from their families and underline both the films' reinforcement of genre-specific conventions as well as their occasional disruption of the audience's expectations.

3 Identity and (Trans)National Spaces

The making of a home is another central aspect in transnational cinema. I have pointed out above that older narratives focus mainly on the question of identity and belonging as it is tied to the immigrants' homeland. The topos of return there receives major emphasis, as do issues such as nostalgia, which has led a number of critics, among them American studies scholar Helena Grice, to characterize the immigrants' original home, i.e. their homeland, as "represent[ing] the past" (212). For Grice, the quest to discover home is hence a search for identity (ibid.). Nevertheless I fear that with this approach towards homeland and identity, one is tempted to fall back into categories of stability and fixity. "The sense of home is the goal of all voyages of self-discovery" is a statement that I no longer consider appropriate (ibid.). In the transnational world, it is not the destination, the settling down, and the arrival at a final home that are significant and that conclude the search for identity. On the contrary, travel itself becomes meaningful. Furthermore, Koshy points out that in the transnational world, identity is produced in various local and global sites and is then no longer restricted to the nation-state the immigrants come from (316). Asian American women do indeed become wanderers, but not in Grice's sense that they are moving toward a final destination, but in Dayal's sense when he speaks of "elective nomadism" (51).

According to Grewal, subjects that are commonly referred to as diasporic or migrant were produced through three discourses of identity: (1) the discourse of the global or universal subject, (2) the national or local subject and (3) the hyphenated or hybrid subject. The global subject was supposed to be stateless, international, and outside of culture, whereas the national subject relied on borders to fashion its identity. The hyphenated or hybrid subject was believed to offer both aspects of resistance and assimilation to the nation-state (36). In her argumentation, the global subject is of major importance, since racial privilege enables it to cross national boundaries, leading to a form of "nomadic power" (43).

The concept of nomadism is elaborated by the feminist philosopher Rosi Braidotti who grounds her thoughts in the theory of the Gilles Deleuze. Deleuze's theory of nomadic subjectivity "stresses the affirmative structure of the subject" (Braidotti, "Nomadism" 305). Deleuze distances himself from stable identities and the notion of roots, arriving at the definition of a subject that continues to change, or, in his words, to "become." In this process, the feminine is the driving force, as it constitutes "the sign of fluid boundaries" (ibid. 307):

> Deleuze conceptualizes woman instead as the constant process of becoming; and in so doing, celebrates the positivity of the non-Oedipal woman, who refuses to function in the procreative socio-symbolic contract of phallocentrism. The non-Oedipal woman remains stubbornly and proudly polymorphous. (ibid. 308)

Ultimately, this grants women the status of self-reflexive subjects who are not to be associated with traditional femininity or, as Braidotti phrases it "woman as constituted in the phallocentric system", i.e. only as "Man's Other" (ibid. 309).

Whereas Deleuze's theory of nomadism focuses on the feminine, Braidotti's theory is initially based on more general thoughts, before she moves on to outline her 'feminist nomadism.' The concept is based on three levels or parts that may at times co-exist. The first is sexual difference conceptualized as difference between man and woman, man being the normative subject and woman the "irrational other" (1994, 160). The second level is concerned with differences among women and aimed at the question of how to "create, legitimate, and respect a multiplicity of alternative forms of feminist subjectivity without falling into relativism" (ibid. 162). The third level finally deals with the conflicts each woman individually faces and analyzes a complex framework of identities and positions. In this argumentation, identity is understood as a dynamic process (ibid. 167). Thus, Braidotti, too, emphasizes a constant state of "in-process" or "becoming" and the affirmation of fluid boundaries, yet goes on to define nomadism as a "strategic re-location in order to rescue what we need of the past in order to trace paths of transformation of our lives here and now" (*Nomadic* 5f.). Obviously, she is not as distanced from the idea of roots as

Deleuze. Instead, subjects need to bear in mind certain aspects of their origin, heritage, and past in order to make sense of their current processes of becoming.

Furthermore, Braidotti is very careful not to confuse the nomad with the migrant or exilic subject. The migrant moves from one place to another with a clear destination in mind, whereas the nomad is characterized by what she calls "nonchalant detachment," because she is able to reject the notion of 'home' altogether (ibid. 20). As a result, dwelling places are consciously selected and the nomad's temporary attachment to them is one determined by choice, rather than by birth, which is the reason why the nomad neither represents homelessness nor a feeling of displacement while longing for home, but abandons "all idea, desire, or nostalgia for fixity" (ibid. 22). In the context of transnational cinema and the films under analysis, these thoughts are of great significance, since they reflect the easiness that the protagonists eventually acquire with respect to traveling and, most importantly, their decreasing attachments to a fixed home that ultimately influences their identity and self-fashioning.

In their work *Cultural Memory and Multiple Identities*, Rüdiger Kunow and Wilfried Raussert study at length the implications of Stuart Hall's argument that "cultural identity encompasses the matter of becoming as well as of being." Identity then is not something that already exists, "transcending place, time, history and culture" (9). In contrast, cultural identity is subject to constant transformation, to the "continuous play of history, culture and power" (ibid.). Furthermore, Hall argues that identity is not an aspect of the past waiting to be recovered and that will, once it is found, secure one's sense of self for all times; instead, identities indicate the ways in which individuals choose to position themselves and are in turn assigned a position (ibid.). Consequently, the contingent and relational nature of identity is highlighted here, too, as well as the power of the subject to fashion its own identity. The following analyses will reveal that space and places – both as non-places and homely places – figure as major influences in the construction of the protagonists' identities.

THE NON-PLACE AS TESTING GROUND

In my chapter on transnational theory I have briefly hinted at the significance of so-called non-places. Theorists argue that they are important in transnational cinema because they constitute the sites of crucial relationship formations. However, secondary literature does not yet offer any explanations as to how these formations are realized and a close reading of the settings in the films aims to shed more light on the question of how identity is fashioned in the non-place.

The term 'non-place' was coined by the anthropologist Marc Augé in 1995 in his seminal study *Non-Places: Introduction to an Anthropology of Supermodernity*. It describes architectural and technological spaces that "cannot be defined as relational or historical or concerned with identity," but are instead "listed, classified, promoted to the status of 'places of memory,' and assigned to a circumscribed and specific position" (77f.). In this respect, Augé lists hospitals, holiday clubs, refugee camps, and supermarkets (78), an enumeration which shows that non-places are meant to be passed through or consumed rather than appropriated and turned into homely places. Non-places need to be understood in opposition to places where orientation and belonging are realized through sedentary and localized inhabitation (Coyne 1). In contrast, they are spaces commonly associated with transit or communication and Augé even goes so far as considering the traveler's space the "archetype of non-place" (86).

Moreover, Emer O'Beirne suggests that non-places are both product and agent of a "contemporary crisis in social relations" and the construction of individual identities (38). This is due to the fact that non-places are capable of "mediat[ing] a whole mass of relations, with the self and with others, which are only indirectly connected with their purpose" (Augé 94). Yet I share Augé's emphasis of words in the mediation of these relations only to some extent (94f.), since sounds and visual imagery are equally part of the processes of mediation. Besides, particularly the characteristic sounds of public announcements, cash registers, airplanes or busy streets immediately trigger associations of non-places. Cinema then lends itself to the close reading of imagery and atmosphere of such non-places and the scenes of *Mississippi Masala* in particular need hardly any dialog to elucidate the family's relationship to the non-place.

Ozan Binici contends that the individual in the non-place is only identified upon entering or leaving and therefore experiences a temporary anonymity while located in the non-place. Consequently, he asserts that individuals temporarily lose their identity in non-places (1), an idea that is very problematic. Binici's thoughts concerning anonymity may be applicable in so far as individuals are rarely identified by others. Since the non-place is a place of transition, travelers move past each other in different directions, without necessarily taking notice of each other. However, I argue that the mere idea that the identity of individuals may not be acknowledged by other travelers does not render it non-existent. Additionally, passing through certain non-places entails stereotyped or generalized categorization: at the airport, for example, travelers experience national categorization with their passport and visa representing their identity and based on their identification they gain or lose access to further stations of their journey.

These issues turn non-places into important settings in transnational cinema. Yet instead of pointing toward identity loss, the characters in the films use non-places as testing grounds for their individual constructs of identity. Seemingly free of history, non-places may enable them to give a voice and form to identity constructs that would remain silent or invisible in homely, appropriated, and settled spaces.

In the three films, the protagonists spend considerable amounts of time in non-places. In *Mississippi Masala*, the motel Monte Christo can certainly be characterizeded as one such non-place. Furthermore, postcolonial studies scholar Simon Featherstone argues that the tourist beach can also be regarded as a non-place (214), for it is a place "where neither otherness nor familiarity holds sway" (ibid. 212). When Mina and Demetrius walk along the beach in Biloxi, he lectures her on the role of tradition: "Traditions are passed down like recipes; you gotta know what to eat and what to leave behind." Later that evening, the two lovers visit the amusement park by the beach. As they ride on one of the whirlygigs, they take turns in exclaiming where they would like to travel. It becomes clear that they both share an enthusiasm for traveling, yet it is not necessarily the destination that matters but the fact of being on the move, which provides a significant cue for the ending of the film. In *Chutney Popcorn*, the food booth on the street deserves attention and I will offer a reading of selected scenes below, whereas in *The Namesake*, the public library may be regarded as a non-place. Though not a place of capitalist consumption, the library is a place to be temporarily visited and is not depicted as a dwelling place, neither for Ashima who works there, nor for any of the people coming there to check out books. With regard to the scope of this study I will limit this section to the analysis of *Mississippi Masala* and *Chutney Popcorn*, since the idea of the non-place as a testing ground for identity and relationship constructions appears most distinctly in these films. Furthermore, the non-places play a crucial role in the plots since they present the settings for scenes which intensify the prevailing conflicts.

Mehta considers the motel in *Mississippi Masala* significant for two reasons. On the one hand, motels are "American" spaces: convenient, inexpensive and linked to working-class life, they constitute rest stops for traveling families or people seeking "illicit sexual encounters" (156). The motel as such carries quite a negative connotation in Hollywood cinema and is a setting for illegal activities, violence and secrecy in films such as the classic 1960 *Psycho* or more recent examples like *Identity* (2003) or *Vacancy* (2007). On the other hand, motels are standardized, thus having the same look, style, and lack of character. For Mehta, the Monte Christo motel is neutral ground (ibid.), an assumption that I find troublesome. The Monte Christo is a problematic place for Mina because her family has attempted to make it their home, thus having turned a place that was meant to be passed through in transit and inhabited only temporarily into a place to stay. In the process, the families have tried to appropriate the place, i.e. fill it with their own identity.

This becomes especially obvious when taking a closer look at Mina's room in the scene in which Jay has just been told that the family has to leave the Monte Christo because Demetrius, in an act of defiance, has decided to sue Anil. Therefore Jay angrily enters Mina's room to confront her. Interestingly, the family does not share one apartment, but Mina has a separate room. The very nature of the motel hence separates the family to some extent from the beginning of their stay. As Jay opens the door, the door to another room is visible behind him, underlining the standardized nature of the motel that sharply contrasts with Mina's personalized room that is crowded with clothes, shoes, hats, and bags in African and Indian fashion. The entrance to her room is framed by a chain of lights in the shape of fish and on the left, a big Bob Marley poster takes up almost one third of the entire frame. Non-western culture is depicted in its traditional form, as well as in the form of popular culture. The colors of the different items dominate over the light and sober colors of Jay's clothes and, interestingly, Bob Marley on the poster is almost bigger than Jay and in general, the long shot of the scene makes him appear less threatening, perhaps also less important. In Mississippi, Mina's family is careful to adopt the Indianness of their relatives; however, Mina's embrace of African, Jamaican, and Western symbols and cultural artifacts distances her from her family. On top of that it becomes clear that she refuses to limit her self-conception to one community and chooses a style that she fashions from experienced culture, traditional heritage, and popular, commodified culture.

Figure 9: Mississippi Masala, *Mina in her room*

The next shot shows Mina from a lower angle on her bed, looking up to face her father and the still elucidates crucial aspects of Mina's identity (see figure 9). Around her, there are different colorful African fabrics on her bed and the wall. The pillows as well as the books and cassette tapes frame Mina's position on the bed, establishing a border between her and Jay. Three items are noteworthy and indicative of the transnational: (1) the globe on her night stand alludes to travels (strikingly India is in the center of the globe facing the camera, yet at the same time also turned away from

Mina), (2) the telephone next to her on the bed illustrates her need to stay connected with a world beyond the motel and (3) the small poster above her bed states "My karma ran over my dogma," implying that her own actions and their outcomes will be more important than authoritative belief and practice.

All in all, the scene refutes Binici's approach to identity loss in non-places, since especially Mina's room mirrors the ways in which she tries to define her identity. Although she has adopted various parts of her father's identity, her room evinces that there is also a great distance between them and that Mina values her own interests. Besides, the mise-en-scène in this scene underscores the conflict between the home space she has fashioned for herself and a life on the move. When Mina yells at her parents "I am still here. Stuck here," as they confront her about her relationship to Demetrius, viewers learn that her home is also conceived as a confinement. Moreover, it needs to be highlighted that, for her, the motel presents simply a means to an end, because she works there and plans on working in motels to make a living with Demetrius.

Furthermore, the sexual relationships in *Mississippi Masala* all take place in motel rooms, thus affirming the connotation that motels are settings for sexual encounters: Chanda and Anil, too, live in the motel and when Mina and Demetrius secretly travel to Biloxi, they also stay at a motel. Comparing the two rooms, one will find that they are quite different. Whereas the Monte Christo seems "chintzy" (157), as Metha phrases it (thus contradicting her own argument of the neutral ground), the motel in Biloxi gives a more sophisticated impression. In Biloxi, the viewer does not see anything of the motel room until Mina and Demetrius wake up in the morning, because before that, the camera work has been focused solely on close-ups of their bodies. In the morning, the room appears clean and bright and the only personal items there are the couple's clothes. Nevertheless, Binici's argument of anonymity in non-places fails here, too, as my analysis in the previous chapter has revealed that the motel room in Biloxi is a site for intimate encounters. I especially want to draw attention to the scene in which Demetrius sings "Happy Birthday" to Mina. "Happy birthday, dear ...Mina," Demetrius whispers. The short pause is striking and heightens the tension of this scene because Demetrius has forgotten her name twice before. Nodding and smiling while he utters it this time, Demetrius stresses that now he knows who she is and values her as an equal partner, instead of an acquaintance he can use in order to make his ex-girlfriend jealous.

Chutney Popcorn exemplifies another important aspect of non-places when the Indian vendor who occupies a street corner with his food booth is regarded as a non-place. Repeatedly, Sarita and Reena pass by there, either together, or each with their mother Meenu and as the plot develops, the nameless vendor becomes witness to their changing relationships and future ideals. Located on the side-walk between the street and the Indian food market, the vendor's booth occupies an intermediary position. His booth is a place where Reena's lesbian identity clashes with her sister's ideal of a heteronormative family. Here, too, the place serves as a testing ground for their new relationships, as they talk about them in front of the vendor while he prepares the food they order, before they put them into practice. It is important that the vendor himself is not asked to participate; however, he does silently judge them, as medium-close ups of his face reveal.

The vendor appears for the first time shortly after Sarita's and Mitch's wedding when they are trying to have a baby, but seem to have difficulties. The establishing shot locates the booth in the Indian neighborhood of New York and Indian music is mixed with synthesizer and beats to create a spherical, though modern and cheesy sound. Close-ups depict the vendor's food-stained hands taking a leaf from a pot, putting various spices and sauces on it and folding it carefully. The process of preparing the snack has almost ritualistic qualities with every step being carefully exercised and the vendor is thus introduced as new cultural authority to the film. After he has stuffed the snack into his mouth, the camera distances to film the food booth from afar as Sarita and her mother approach. Before they even reach the counter, Meenu orders their food in Hindi, thus acknowledging the vendor's cultural authority.

Although the vendor wears the same clothes in each scene, hence giving the impression of stability, the camera perspective changes each time the women approach the booth. The first time, the camera films the women from behind. Meenu, waiting for their food, has her back turned to the camera, while Sarita is standing with her back toward the vendor, only turning her head to speak to her mother. After they have received their food, they remain in front of the booth and discuss the delicate subject. The second time the vendor's booth is shown, an establishing shot shows Sarita waiting at a street corner for her sister, fittingly standing under a one-way-street sign which illustrates that their path, once they start, allows no turning back. The same music accompanies the vendor's hands as they move across the counter, this time to produce several pieces of food with the same ingredients. The camera views both the girls and the vendor's arms from outside the booth (see figure 10).

Figure 10: Chutney Popcorn, *Reena and Sarita at the vendor's booth*

Through this perspective, the sisters are separated by the vertical post of the booth, a visual composition that underlines the distance of their thoughts: Whereas Reena continues to offer to have the baby for her sister, Sarita dismisses the idea as nonsense. "Maybe I wasn't meant to have a baby," she wearily states. Here the camera perspective changes to include point-of-view shots of the girls and the vendor, suggesting interaction and exchange and hence alluding to the women's struggle with their ideas of tradition and normativity. However, the fact that he folds his arms and casts a judgmental look at them makes it clear that from his standpoint, both their idea and Sarita's inability to give birth are to be viewed critically.

During the third encounter, Sarita is already waiting at the booth, eating, while Reena comes running at her, waving her positive pregnancy test. Now the camera films the sisters from behind the counter, a perspective that brings them physically closer together. Arora convincingly argues that by privileging the bond between mothers and daughters, as well as between the two sisters, masculinist and heterosexist assumptions of the diaspora are disrupted (38). They do not take any notice of the vendor, only Reena looks at him shortly and drags her sister away from the booth when Sarita exclaims: "You have not menstruated?" The comically sounding exclamation emphasizes Reena's active choice to become pregnant, yet this choice is not to be further discussed in the presence of the vendor. The camera movement throughout these three scenes therefore illustrates the girls' relationship to cultural and traditional authority. While at first the camera is on their side, in tune with Sarita as she is desperate to fulfill others' expectations, it gradually moves to the other side as they decide on an alternative plan. Now, when the plan is finalized through Reena's confirmed pregnancy, the camera is in opposition to them.

In a fourth encounter Meenu has just found out that Reena is pregnant and intends to keep the baby. She walks quickly along the street, Sarita to her right and Reena to her left, each furious and not returning the other's gaze. However, instead of stopping for a snack, they keep walking past the booth, leaving the vendor, who is already stretching out his arm to hand over the usual order, clueless. As a comical side-kick, he provides a brief moment of comic relief in the tense situation but Meenu's rejection of the vendor's food has further implications. What is more important is that toward the end of the plot, when Reena and her mother start developing a more intimate and reconciling relationship and address the subject of homosexuality openly, Meenu does not buy food at the booth, but brings it along in a box, thus circumventing an encounter with the vendor. The women are now depicted as self-reliant and at ease with Reena's and Sarita's choices and turning away from cultural authorities.

SUBVERTING THE SUBURBAN DREAM

Like the non-place, suburbia, too, is a highly charged setting which appears in each of the films. A significant American symbol, suburbia bears close connections to the American Dream, whose ideological forces have operated on both Americans and immigrants for generations. In his seminal critiques of suburban space, sociologist Bennett Berger has repeatedly referred to suburbia as a myth that spurs the image of a classless and homogenous society in which ethnicity remains invisible but in which "the marvelous productivity of American industry" looms large:

> the ranch house with the occupied two-car garage, the refrigerator and freezer, the washer and dryer, the garbage disposal and the built-in range and dishwasher, the color TV and the hi fi stereo. Suburbia: its lawns trim, its driveways clean, its children happy on its curving streets and in its pastel schools. Suburbia [...] is America. (85f.)

In this vein, suburban space is intricately intertwined with symbols, such as the two-car garage, that signify middle-class life and it is particularly the ownership of a suburban house that is indicative of social status (cf. also Smukler 1).

Making a home in suburbia therefore represents the achievement of a goal – the American Dream – and the endpoint of a journey. Moving to suburbia thus symbolizes assimilation to the American way of life and, accordingly, purchasing a house in the suburbs links the buyer's identity inextricably to the new home, an issue that I have problematized above. Despite the fact that this stands in stark contrast to abandoning fixed home spaces in the transnational world, in the films, viewers encounter numerous signifiers of suburbia, among them lawnmowers, station wagons, and barbecues (Berger 82), and on first sight, the three films seem to subscribe to the tradition of depicting suburbia as an idyllic place. In all films, the home in the suburbs not only symbolizes the American way of life, but is always a family place and media studies scholar Maya Smukler is certainly correct when she observes that the suburban landscape is a place for the family *per se* since such houses are not to be purchased by singletons (3). Although familial troubles are frequently part of the storylines of filmic representations of suburbia, these conflicts are ultimately solved to underline not only the harmony within the respective family, but also reinforce the cohesion of suburbia at large (ibid.). Suburbia therefore stands in for continuity and stability and is a space where the heteronormative is in place.

As I will show here, the films do employ such symbolism, yet their construction of the characters' suburban lives and homes significantly goes beyond that. After all, ethnic differences do not disappear in the film's suburbs, thus undermining the myth that, as Berger outlines, the suburb may serve as a melting pot for all sorts of social and racial differences (83f.). Notably, the plots also depart from idyllic representations of suburban life. Nair's and Ganatra's films to not go so far as drafting a suburbia that is, according to historians Becky Nicolaides and Andrew Viese, a "cesspool for every American neurosis and social pathology" (291), as becomes evident in films like *The Truman Show* (1998) and *Pleasantville* (1998), as well as in TV series such as *Desperate Housewives* (2004–2012) and the recent sitcom *Suburgatory* (2011–2014), yet they do highlight the oppressive force of suburbia.

In *Mississippi Masala*, Mina is invited to the birthday party of Demetrius's grandfather. She becomes a guest in a setting in which the values of the Williams family are carefully accentuated. While the men are outside preparing the BBQ, Aunt Rose and Mina prepare food in the kitchen; there Aunt Rose tells Mina that Demetrius turned down the opportunity to go to college in order to stay with his father, revealing the significance of a strong tie between the members of their family. However, Aunt Rose also points out that Demetrius did not stay in Greenwood because he wanted to: Much like Mina imagines the motel as a confinement, he, too, feels confined in the suburban space.

Suburbia as a space of the heteronormative appears even more dominantly in *Chutney Popcorn* and *The Namesake*. In *Chutney Popcorn*, Sarita's and Mitch's wedding takes place in what Arora calls "white picket-fence suburbia" (36). She suggests that, since the guests do not mind that "their music, clothes, dance, food or other customs" may be considered strange by the dominant group, suburbia loses its connection with "backyard America." In other words, suburbia as the quintessentially American space is denied its normative associations (Aurora ibid.). Although Arora's statement is true to some extent, it is also quite problematic, for despite the fact that suburbia may not be considered emblematic of white America anymore, since it is as much home to the ethnic as to the white population, it does maintain a sense of the normative, which is what I aim to illustrate in this section.

A theme that strikes viewers in the film in connection to suburbia is the theme of gardening. Both Sarita and Mitch seem to be constantly occupied with taking care of their backyard. Women's studies scholar Mary Bryson explains the cultural significance of gardening as follows:

> Modern culture is a garden culture. It defines itself as the design for an ideal life and a perfect arrangement of human conditions. It constructs its own identity out of distrust of nature. In fact, it defines itself and nature, and the distinction between them, through its endemic distrust of spontaneity and its longing for a better, and necessarily artificial, order. (1)

It is Sarita's distrust, if not even contempt, for nature which becomes apparent when she is in her garden. In the first scene, Reena and Sarita are kneeling next to each other in the garden and planting a flower. The color of the flower – red – may be understood as an allusion to fertility as well, especially since most of its buds are still closed. Whereas Reena wears gloves, her sister is working with her bare hands, vigorously, almost pushing her sister's hand away, aiding the impression that that it is very important for her to plant the flower herself. "It never occurred to me that I couldn't have children," Sarita then states while still looking down at the flower and covering the hole they have dug with dirt and the films therefore powerfully links gardening to Sarita's and Mitch's procreation, or, to be more precise, Sarita's agency in the process.

In the ensuing dialogue the verbal cues parallel the visual narration, for when Reena avers that she would like to help, her sister replies: "There is nothing you can do." The flowerbed hence symbolizes Sarita's womb and the flower she struggles to plant by herself a "seed" and fertility. Reena, however, persists, maintaining: "There is something I can do. I can have the baby for you." Reena's perspective is shown in point-of-view shots of her sister, yet her sister does not return the gaze through the camera: instead, a shot that looks over Sarita's head focuses on Reena indicating that Sarita does not want to become engaged in her sister's idea at the beginning. Only when Reena moves on to tell her sister details of her idea is there more interaction between them.

Furthermore, this scene elucidates that gardening is not only used as an attempt to uphold an image of beauty and harmony on the outside, but also to convey the idea of creating something artificial. Nature fails Sarita, since her body does not allow her to reproduce biologically, yet her sister offers a way to bypass Sarita's condition by suggesting that she could have the baby and then give it to her sister. Discontent about nature is uttered at the same time Sarita is trying to improve nature around her home as she arranges the flowers in a line next to the garden walk as to create order and life.

In the second scene in their suburban backyard, Sarita tells Mitch about her sister's offer. She sits in a garden chair, while her husband is raking leaves. Behind him, the quiet street and the trees of the neighborhood can be seen and the only sound in the background is the sound of a lawnmower, underlining the theme of gardening. Sarita remains seated with a book and notes in her hands and casually tells Mitch

[...] we just did the usual gardening stuff. [...] You know my sister, she disappears to the store for an hour and then comes back with some crazy idea about being a surrogate mother. Can you believe her? She thought she could help, by, you know, having the baby for us.

Since she continues to take notes one gains the impression that the words have little significance for her and are merely a "crazy idea" that Sarita has already dismissed. Mitch, on the other hand, stops raking and looks up from the ground to face his wife. The point-of-view shots which then follow suggest interaction as Mitch starts thinking about the advantages of Reena having their baby. The film hence uses the theme of gardening to gradually subvert heteronormativity.

Whereas Mina's family in *Mississippi Masala* does not fit the stereotype of the successful immigrant, the story of Ashima and Ashoke in *The Namesake* illustrates the immigrants' striving for a prosperous life (Mehta 156). For the Ganguli family, moving from the inner city into the suburbs is connected to the pursuit of the American Dream. However, Natalie Friedman rightly argues that the plot extends well beyond the mere pursuit of the American Dream and suggests that the idea of assimilation is no longer the center of the immigrant story. Instead, the film focuses on what happens once this dream is achieved (112).

First of all, I would like to take a closer look at the scene in which the family has just moved to suburbia. The establishing shot shows a big tree with red leaves. It is fall and the neighborhood is introduced as an idyllic place away from the noisy city. Moreover, the shot shows that their house is located in a cul-de-sac, thus emblematic of the so-called 'suburban dream,' an idea that responds to needs of quiet and safety (Nielsen n.p.). In their study *Tomorrow's Cities, Tomorrow's Suburbs*, urban studies scholars William Lucy and David Phillis argue that the cul-de-sac "embodies desires by residents to control their physical setting," because trespassing and unwanted traffic, for example, are shut out (249). Hence the cul-de-sac is generally an isolated space. John Nielsen adds that houses were built so that their windows only looked out to the front and back, but not to the sides (n.p.). This way, privacy is valued highly and at the same time, the family home as designed to be presentable.

In the context of the film, the new house in suburbia illustrates the family's improving economic status, as well as perhaps their own desire for a stable and safe place. Nevertheless, their move into the new house should not be read as an attempt to assimilate: "Welcome to suburbia," one of Ashoke's Indian friends exclaims as the perspective changes to a long shot that shows the three Indian men outside the house talking. The move is a step that the family's friends congratulate them on and since this is the first time the family actually has company, their move also indicates a rise on the social ladder. Against the backdrop of large houses, children are playing in the street and riding their bicycles, two men are working on a car and some others are sitting at the side of the street in garden chairs (see figure 11).

None of the white characters in the shot seems to take any notice of the men and the entire scenery presents idyllic middle-class life. The camera then focuses on the men. As they admire the house, Ashoke states: "Everything is bought in a yard sale. Ashima does not like it, but I say 'What is wrong with it?' Even my chairman who lives in a huge mansion wears a trouser bought for fifty cents." The other men laugh: "That is America, Ashoke." While Ashima is still bewildered by the American way of life, Ashoke is more likely to simply accept certain ideas and the scene thus reveals that the family does not assimilate to American suburban life but remains within their set of values. I therefore do not agree with literary critic

Figure 11: The Namesake, *"Welcome to suburbia"*

John Muir who contends that the second family home in the suburbs elucidates the uniformity of urban development (236). Quite to the contrary, the first scene in their home shows that even though the house may look American on the outside, inside, Indian tradition looms large, for the family celebrates their daughter Sonia's naming ceremony, a traditional Hindu ritual, in the company of other Indian friends and relatives.

Although the family has been aspiring to a house of their own for a long time and the new home initially carries positive connotations, it repeatedly becomes the setting of traumatic encounters. Shortly after they have moved in, the family receives the news that Ashima's father has died. Later, after they return from their vacation in India, they find that their postbox has been sprayed and vandalized in an act of racism. The most important scene, though, takes place when Ashima learns that Ashoke has died while teaching in Ohio. All alone in the big, empty, and dark house, she turns on all the lights so as to make the house seem less eerie. Finally she runs outside and collapses crying in the garden. A long shot depicts the house and the yard to reveal the full tragedy of the situation: It is around Christmas and the family has put up Christmas lights and reindeers on the lawn. So the image of the peaceful garden, emblematic of an approaching joyful time, becomes the setting of Ashima's greatest sorrow and foreshadows her decision to leave the house, one of the issues I will discuss in the final chapter when I analyze the endings of the films.

4 HAPPILY EVER AFTER?

In earlier Asian American narratives, the trope of return was featured as an imagined or actual end-point to the action that allowed for a resolution of the dilemma of identification (Koshy 340). Ultimately, the aforementioned "either/or" perception of identity is at the center of these narratives. Since this construction can no longer grasp the complexities and paradoxes of cultural belonging, transnational narratives call for a different ending. Koshy correctly notes that they "deliberately avoid closure" and end with their characters beginning a new journey, in transit, or on the road (ibid.): *Mississippi Masala* ends with Mina and Demetrius deciding that they will travel together in order to make a living and the film closes with depictions of the reunited couple against the background of vast fields and open roads. At the same time, Jay has briefly returned to Uganda to find the homeland he yearned for dramatically changed, which prompts him to abandon the plan for the family's return to Africa. Although the characters in *Chutney Popcorn* do find closure to some extent when the family is restructured after the baby's birth, the film leaves viewers with an ambiguous ending. In *The Namesake*, Ashima decides to sell the house and divide her time between India and the United States in order to be able to both spend time with her grown-up children and their families and to pursue her passion of singing again, hence choosing a life on the move.

As films are sites for the negotiation of meaning, they also employ contradicting points of view that simultaneously work through and contain anxieties of various kinds. Thus they have the potential to subvert issues, while re-inscribing them at other times (Stanford Friedman 27). Likewise, transnational cinema both undermines and co-opts American exceptionalism, thus creating an "optimistic and occasionally utopian picture of racially mixed societies" (Seshagiri 181). In a similar vein, the following statement by postcolonial studies scholar Gerhard Stilz praises the possibilities that sequences of resistance and reconciliation may provide, yet remains suspicious in tone:

The sequence "resistance and reconciliation" sounds pleasant and inviting. In a mythical inclusivity, it promises to recognize and heal fissures, identify and reverse alienation, and soothe skepticism and controversies in a diverging world. "Resistance and reconciliation" names a process that can and needs to be achieved amongst rational, deliberate, and civilized human beings. It is balm for the clefts and abysses of the diversification of modernity and the glue that can aid in joining together and making sense of the free play of what has been rendered senseless by postmodernity. (51; my translation)

This is precisely the point where scholarship divides into appraisal and harsh criticism. With regard to *Mississippi Masala*, African-American studies scholar Adeleke Adeeko, on the one hand, believes that the positive resonance of the ending makes the film worthy of praise (132). Mina and Demetrius, he argues, are "fortified," while individuals who attempt to stall the realization of their will to create relationships that can successfully overcome cultural restrictions seem to fail in the end. According to him, the films encourage cultural mixing (ibid.). Desai, on the other hand, asserts that the idea that Africa and India cease to be "out there" but are now located within American borders underlines the "domesticating tendency of U.S. multiculturalism" and an exceptionalist feeling of "we are the world" (88). Not only does this approach fail to acknowledge the transnational setting, but it also suggests American exceptionalism when it turns America into the setting in which national identities are seemingly overcome (ibid. 90).

Finally, the strongest critique of *Mississippi Masala* is uttered by scholar-activist bell hooks and postcolonial studies scholar Anuradha Dingwaney:

[The film's] too apparent multicultural virtue is troubling not just because it simplistically turns a specifically American yearning for honest interracial relationships into a global concern but primarily for concealing the devious role of the centers of (post)colonial and imperial domination [...] that force the two lovers into the cultural conflicts they are left alone to resolve: "The American dream of a love that triumphs over politics is a negation of our need to seriously examine the West's relationship to India, Africa, and global liberation movements for national freedom and self-determination." (quoted in Adeeko 132)

Hence they consider the film's approval of American exceptionalism as an attempt to generalize one nation's problem (ibid.). So in the following sections I will analyze the endings of all three films with respect to the issues of mobility, family relationships, and the critique that they constitute utopian visions.

NOMADISM AND MOBILITY

According to Bill Ashcroft, all texts of the Indian diaspora show two poles which comprise the landscape of identity: "the pole of memory" and "the pole of possibility." These poles are symbolic of two generations of writers, in which directors Mira Nair and Nisha Ganatra should be considered members of the second generation that is concerned with the aspect of "possibility" (15). He adds that these writers fashion settings whose major characteristic is mobility (16). However, at the same time, one should not neglect the fact that the trope of mobility is intertwined with the American idea of the open road and field (Desai 95).

Seshagiri aptly states that *Mississippi Masala* is a film about departures, not arrivals (192). As the family leaves Uganda, young Mina turns to her father and asks "Where are we going? [...] When are we coming back?" – two questions that are never answered. Besides, the map during the opening credits traces their journey and England becomes only a transitory point. Likewise, their "home" in Mississippi is the motel Monte Christo, which I have referred to above, and Jay's eager attempts to retrieve his passport and return to Uganda illustrate that their home in the U.S., too, may be only transitory. Yet whereas the film suggests that Jay will eventually settle permanently in Greenwood, Mina leaves her family to be with Demetrius. As they leave, they do not know their destination themselves; once again, the focus is not on an arrival, but on the moment of departure which ends the film, and, more importantly, on the subsequent journey the final shots foreshadow, something Seshagiri terms "nomadic vision of togetherness" (ibid.).

Toward the end, the crises in *Mississippi Masala* have been exacerbated: Anil has told Jay that he will no longer tolerate their presence at the family's motel, while Demetrius faces the failure of his business, since neither motel owners nor the bank or the chamber of commerce will continue to support him. On top of that, he and Mina are not speaking to each other anymore as Demetrius holds her family responsible for his financial situation. The plot shows that not only the solidarity amongst people of color has faded, but that also severe racist arguments begin to surface. Interestingly, Jay does not consider Anil's words problematic: "I was thinking about going anyway. This was just what we needed." It is Jay's decision to go back to Uganda, yet here he speaks for his wife and daughter, too. For the first time since they have been in Mississippi, Jay claims back his status as the head of the family. At least to him the idea of leaving is empowering in so far as it transforms another experience of expulsion. At this point in the plot, Mina is convinced that she will join her family in Uganda, confirming Jay's authority that has not allowed for any discussion. This is also revealed in her short conversation with Demetrius's father Williben: "I didn't come to make trouble. I just want to say goodbye to him [Demetrius]. We're moving back to Africa."

Nevertheless, she steals away from the Monte Christo secretly. As soon as she is out of sight, she runs for Anil's car. Dust stirs and the tires screech when she drives off, and her journey is therefore initiated by a rash escape. The following scene depicts her driving around in order to find Demetrius, barely able to control the car. When she has found him and he ignores her, she chases him until he turns into a gas station and confronts her: "You walk into my life from all these fancy places and I know I'm just a little carpet cleaner and I ain't never left Mississippi, but I was happy. I was happy where I was until you came along after me." Obviously, he reproaches her for destroying the business that took him years to establish. Not only did this business provide him with a sense of security and stability, it also elevated his status in Greenwood. Demetrius is a self-made man, but this scene exposes that having a business of his own has not made him independent, but tied him to various obligations.

The question that I wish to raise is why Mina changes her mind and decides not to return to Uganda with her family, but to travel with Demetrius. A simple answer may be that at the time the family prepares to leave the Monte Christo, Mina considers the relationship failed. With no other ties or friendships, she is bound to follow her parents. When Demetrius confesses that although initially he used her to make his ex-girlfriend jealous, he eventually did fall in love with her, she changes her mind. On the meta-level, however, one may also argue that Mina has come to understand the irreversibility of migrancy (Adeeko 140). In other words, she cannot go back but has to keep moving forward and continue her journey:

Mississippi Masala turns to mobility and the heterosexual mixed-race romance as a resolution to displacement and exclusion. It shifts discourses of diaspora from an emphasis on a return to homeland to a refusal and replacement of the homeland in favor of diaspora as the frontier. [...] It succumbs to the myth of a 'home on the range' – both Western frontier home and a home within constant movement. This narrative of the home on the range is grounded in narratives of American exceptionalism, expansion and imperialism. (Desai 73)

The conversation that follows takes place at the side of the road and centers on the idea of movement. Although the background behind the characters is blurred, the shots illustrate the vast open range behind them. The road is visible in each shot, indicating movement that is underlined as a car rushes past. As the camera shows Mina and Demetrius sitting on the hood of Anil's car, not facing each other, she asks: "What are you going to do now?" and he answers: "Well, Tyrone went to Los Angeles. I am thinking about going somewhere I guess." "Demetrius, can I come with you?" Mina gets up and faces him. A medium long-shot from the side shows him still sitting on the car, while she is standing in front of him and thus meets him at eye level. On the one hand this position suggests that they are now interacting again on a more personal level, with Demetrius being forced to look at her. Additionally, they are now the same size, a position that symbolizes equality. On the other hand, this shot also illustrates that Mina is ready to leave; Demetrius, in contrast, stays put, as their dialogue underlines:

Demetrius:	"Come with me where?"
Mina:	"I don't know, wherever you're going."
Demetrius:	"I wasn't saying I was going anywhere, I said I was thinking about it."
Mina:	"Well, think about it. You said we're going to travel and see the world and ..."
Demetrius:	"Yeah, what are we gonna live on? Fresh air?"
Mina:	"No, you've got the van. I could be your partner. I know how to clean rooms."
Demetrius:	"You're out of your mind, you know that?"
Mina:	"I'm not out of my mind. It's crazy to stay here."

Demetrius is still vague about his plans and has not made a decision yet. His question about the "where" of his journey makes it clear that he needs a destination before he can begin traveling, like Tyrone who is headed for Los Angeles. Mina, on the contrary, is more concerned about leaving and will go "wherever." Her idea to "travel and see the world" points to continuous movement. By voicing what Demetrius has only been thinking about, Mina takes action and decides for them. Ultimately Demetrius's attempt to ridicule her and expose the idea as naiveté fails. Yet he still regards the idea as absurd and goes on to mention that the van does not even belong to him, but will be taken away by the bank soon. Furthermore, he states that they will get into trouble once they cross the state border. Demetrius is caught in fixed structures and confined by boundaries, but Mina pushes these thoughts aside: "That's two weeks away."

Interestingly, their discussion does not focus on the question of love and relationship, even though Demetrius has confessed his honest love only seconds earlier. The future they now discuss is based on the assumption that they can become equal partners who both work for their living as they travel. It is here that *Mississippi Masala* pointedly departs from the script of the Hollywood romantic comedy that would satisfy the audience's expectation of an affectionate reunion. This expectation is disrupted by the lovers' focus on their coming journey, which attributes great significance to their life on the move.

In the next shot, it has already become dark, but Mina and Demetrius are still at the gas station, now ready to tell their parents that they will leave together. First Demetrius calls his father Williben at work, who understands: "I knew there was something that's been keeping you from being happy." Finally, Williben states that he can take care of himself, hence releasing Demetrius from one of his obligations that have kept him tied to Greenwood. Their conversation is ended by Mrs. Morgan who calls from the off for Williben to return to work. "Stay in touch," Williben says and when Demetrius ends with "I love you," he replies "God bless you, son," ending their conversation on a strong and positive note.

When Demetrius hangs up the phone, thunder is becoming louder and rain sets in, signifying the climactic moment of the plot as Mina then calls the motel (see figure 12). Standing in the phone booth, she is surrounded by rain and the water runs down the glass, making her tears more dramatic.

Figure 12: Missippi Masala, *Mina's phone call*

With Girgus I hold that the phone call signifies proximity and distance at the same time (37). Even though the family is connected, the phone call constitutes the construction of a new reality on Mina's part and "she could be calling from a different world" (ibid. 36). This is also emphasized by the triadic relationship across the telephone connecting Mina, Kinnu and Jay, each in separate places. As soon as Jay hears that Mina is with Demetrius, he puts the phone down, not accepting of his daughter's relationship to the Black man. "Ma, I'm not coming back. I'm sorry, but I can't go to Uganda. What would I do there?" Obviously, Uganda is no longer a home for her and, besides, Ann Kaplan correctly maintains that it is impossible to return to a home that one has left, since it has become a purely imaginary fixed space (173), which is why Mina has to move on. It is significant that Mina demands to know from her parents what she should do in Uganda, because although she does not know what they are going to do once they leave Mississippi either, she seems to feel that she has the agency to create something by herself.

Mina's voice is shaky and undoubtedly it is hard for her to utter these words. Yet in contrast to her dramatic and violent escape, the telephone conversation strikes a reconciliatory tone:

Mina:	"We're leaving Mississippi to see what we can do."
Kinnu:	"We'll talk about it. But come back home now."
Mina:	"I can't. If I don't leave now, I'll never leave. You know that."
Kinnu:	"Then promise me something. Ring Jammubhai every two days and tell him where you are."
Mina:	"Mum, I'll see you soon, ok? Kiss papa for me."

Whereas Kinnu still tries to mediate the situation, Mina is determined to put her plan into action. When she tells her mother that she knows the situation, Kinnu suddenly changes her mind and their exchange stresses the bond between mother and daughter. Without further explanation, Kinnu understands Mina's problem. However, at the same time, the conversation also illustrates a generational difference: Kinnu has chosen to stay, while Mina is now uncompromising in her decision to leave.

Yet Kinnu's plea to ring uncle Jammubhai every other day is quite ambiguous. Why should Mina call her relatives and not her parents? On the one hand, Kinnu may still be assuming that she and Jay will be leaving for Uganda soon, where Mina may not be able to reach them, thus she is supposed to ring their relatives. On the other hand, considering the problematic relationship that Mina had to her relatives, Kinnu's request seems odd. It certainly shows her desire to stick to fixed locales: Mina is not asked to call and tell them how she is, but where she is. To an extent, Jammubhai will then remain in control of her. In previous sections I have characterized Mina's family and relatives as representatives of a traditional life-style which symbolizes the push and pull between tradition and self-definition. Mina does not reply to her mother's request, but simply moves on to end the conversation and her reaction leaves open whether or not she will continue to keep in touch with her relatives at the motel.

Like Demetrius's conversation with Williben, Mina's conversation with Kinnu does not end with a "goodbye," but with a declaration of love. The separation from their families that is dramatized by the aesthetics of the film finally receives a hint of approval (in the case of Williben) or at least understanding (Kinnu). The fact that a "goodbye" is not uttered elucidates that their separation may not be permanent, something that is confirmed by Mina's "see you soon." The following shot depicts the motel room in which Kinnu and Jay are facing each other. The sound of the rain can still be heard, as well as soft classical Indian music. Kinnu attempts to explain their daughter's leaving to Jay by saying: "She has a mind of her own. She can't grow here anymore. Mina is your daughter, she's like you." With this explanation, Kinnu not only re-establishes the bond between father and daughter, but strengthens the familial ties as such by confirming that Mina is indeed Jay's daughter.

Desai purports that the ending of *Mississippi Masala* is a celebration of the "liberation of self-employment in the service-industry" that, together with the interracial relationship, turns economic disenfranchisement into a happy ending. The Third World woman, she claims, is incorporated into the global economy (87). Considering the fact that Demetrius's business slogan reads "your dirt is our bread and butter," though, Desai's argument loses some of its validity. The two young business people may find a place in the economic structures, however, only at the very bottom of the social ladder in the working class, living of what others reject.

Mobility is also an important theme in *Chutney Popcorn*. According to Arora, not only mehndi but also Reena's motorcycle serve to bridge physical and emotional distances between her biological and her chosen, lesbian, family (35). While the motorcycle initially situates Reena in the role of an outsider in her Indian community, for instance when she arrives late for Sarita's wedding ceremony, it later develops into a handy means to connect Sarita's home in the suburb to Reena's inner city apartment. More than that, the motorcycle is stripped of its Hollywood connotations of white masculine heterosexuality and instead becomes a trope in Ganatra's film which signifies queerness as well as diasporic movement:

> The effects of this movement are felt not only by the "body that travels," but also by the bodies that are "encountered," and spaces and places traversed are also transformed in the traffic. Reena's movement between "officially designed spaces" – the ethnic diaspora, New York City neighborhoods, suburban or urban spaces, chic parlors or "unfashionable" grocery stores, Hindu rituals – remaps all of these territories, even as Reena's own identity is formed in the interstices of these places. (Arora 35)

Finally, the motorcycle becomes an important symbol of the changing relationship between the sisters and their respective conceptions of identity, tradition, and choice, as becomes evident in the scenes in which Reena and

Sarita ride the motorcycle. Sarita is depicted riding the motorcycle for the first time when she has just learnt that she cannot become pregnant. Sitting behind her sister, she holds on to her and leans against her, as if looking for consolation. The fact that neither of them wears a helmet in this scene allows them to be closer to each other. Apart from this, their faces are visible and at the center of the medium shot, which adds to the intimate atmosphere of the scene. The scene is accompanied by Indian music, thus associating the women's travels with the Indian diaspora and stressing Sarita's strong adherence to Indian traditions and her resulting devastation over the fact that she cannot bear a child.

When Reena's first attempts to become pregnant fail, Mitch starts blaming her continuous use of the motorcycle. He receives a call of which the viewer can only hear his side of the conversation: "Oh, so the motorcycle can be affecting this" he states before he hangs up. His utterance "I was right, the motorcycle has to go" indicates that they may have talked about it earlier. Since he carries on moving the sofa as though nothing happened, he is unaware of the significance the motorcycle has for Reena. Losing the bike would of course deprive Reena of the ability to alternate between the different spaces and it would also deprive her of a part of her lesbian identity.

However, it is not Mitch who finally takes the motorcycle away, but Reena decides to give it up herself. Until then she has continued to ride her motorcycle even as she has learned that she is actually pregnant and only when Sarita, still mad at her, argues "look at you, you're gonna be a mother," does Reena's attitude change. As she leaves her sister's front yard and goes to her bike, she notices her reflection in a car parked next to it. She then turns to the car and looks at herself from the side, a perspective that emphasizes her growing belly, touches it and smoothes down her shirt in order to see it even better. The composition of the frame places her reflection in the car at the center, since the motorcycle, the car, and Reena's body are cut off. The reflection she sees in the car is naturally a distorted one, so that the image that she conceives of herself is somewhat distorted, too, showing her rather an extreme than an actual image.

Right when she notices her reflection, the same rock song as during the wedding reception sets in, again underlining the push and pull that Reena is going through. At the beginning, she decided to leave the reception and return to her lesbian chosen family. Now, however, she chooses to give up the bike and carefully pushes it into Sarita's garage, covers it, looks at it once more, as if bidding farewell to it and then closes the garage door before she walks away. By closing the door behind her, she completes her separation from the bike and an establishing shot shows her new mode of transportation, the subway. Nevertheless, the atmosphere in the subway, in which she is depicted as sitting by herself driving through the dark, is gloomy. A point-of-view shot illustrates that she has noticed an advertisement for prenatal care, thus becoming more acquainted, but maybe not more comfortable, with her new role as a mother.

In the next scene she tries to apply henna to Lisa's body, but can produce only thick and sloppy lines. It becomes clear that at this point, her giving up the motorcycle is only an unsatisfying compromise. Nevertheless, it is not enough to simply view this in terms of giving up mobility, as Grewal reminds us that the "binaries of mobility and immobility" are not useful anymore to answer the question of belonging, since in the transnational world, the ability to connect signifies that mobility as such can no longer remain a salient issue (11). The question of mobility or immobility therefore always has to be tied to the observation of how it impacts the protagonist's self-conception. Reena, now also facing a conflict with her lesbian friends who accuse her of "perpetuat[ing] the heterosexual family model," is now an outsider in both of her communities, which brings the conflicts to a climactic point.

Arora argues that, while the riders change, the bike still remains a symbol of queer diasporic movement (35). This is significant in the scene in which Sarita walks into the garage, uncovers the motorcycle and climbs on it without hesitation. She tries until she has found a firm grip on the handles and otherwise seems comfortable on the bike still mounted on the kickstand and thus unable to move. Unnoticed, Mitch enters the garage behind her and when she does see him, she seems shy and does not want to meet his gaze long. The fact that he climbs on the motorcycle behind her illustrates that he is willing to support her. He embraces her tightly, yet her hands remain on the handles and she closes her eyes only for a short time, overwhelmed and surprised by the situation. It is striking that they end their dispute about Reena's pregnancy at this point, with Mitch acknowledging her attempt to embrace a part of Reena's life, namely her agency and the autonomous choices she makes. The non-diegetic music, another rock song, connects Sarita in this scene with her sister and Arora adds that Sarita "starts to make her journey beyond the hetero-normal" (ibid.).

The first time Sarita rides the bike herself is while Reena is giving birth to the baby. Although her look is tense, her movement, which is filmed from left to right, denotes progress. Finally, before the end of the plot, Sarita stops with the bike in front of the beauty parlor, yet remains sitting on it and keeps the engine running. As she looks back over her shoulder, point-of-view shots show Sarita and Reena smiling at each other, apparently understanding without words. By picking up the motorcycle, Sarita has changed roles with her sister and has come to understand Reena's life and choices (Arora 36). While Sarita is now depicted as moving away, Reena appears to have settled. This may be explained by queer studies scholar Gayatri Gopinath who argues that queer South Asian texts are generally more concerned with "remaking the space of home from within." "Staying put" seems to be a way of remaining within the oppressive structure of the home while reworking its heteronormative logic (14f.).

In contrast, Ashima in *The Namesake* ceases to be content with the idea of staying put. After Ashoke's death, Ashima is desperate. Sitting across from her friend and colleague in the library, she confides in her, with her eyes fixed on her cup of coffee: "It's so hard to know what to do sometimes." The death of her husband has marked her visibly: she looks tired and has dark circles around her eyes and her sari stands away from her shoulders, as if she has lost weight. Her friend replies: "I was looking at this Joseph Campbell book the other day, and he says when you feel lost, you should close your eyes and think of when you were most happy. Not thrilled. Just deeply happy. It's called 'following your bliss.'" As she finishes, Ashima raises her eyebrows and smiles shyly. "You wanna try it?" her friend asks and she nods hardly noticeably, then closes her eyes. When she opens her eyes again, she appears to have made a decision. "I have been thinking about leaving. Is that really selfish of me?" Ashima asks. She does not raise her eyes to face her friend and clearly, the thought is still too daring for her. Only when she states that she believes her children well settled does she look her at her friend and smile again.

Campbell's advice also surfaces in a subsequent scene, when viewers encounter Ashima again, this time in the kitchen preparing food together with Moushumi, her daughter-in-law. When Moushumi asks her whether she does not mind that Ben, Sonia's fiancé, is not Indian, she happily replies: "Times have changed and he makes Sonia very happy. She is following her bliss." – "You've been reading Joseph Campbell," Moushumi remarks and the women laugh together. Apparently both Indian women have turned to American self-help culture to find happiness and the fact that Ashima talks about her daughter in the terms the self-help book uses elucidates that she has already internalized its idea. Numerous theorists have offered analyses of America's preoccupation with self-help books and one of them, Sandra Dolby, argues that self-help books always respond to a lack or problem, thus providing a critique of culture. By highlighting what needs to be changed, these books tend to selectively maintain "what is necessary and deemed good" (11) and accordingly affirm the social system. At the same time, they place a strong focus on the individual (ibid. 20).

Nevertheless, Ashima conceals the influence of the book when she breaks the news to her family in the following scene:

Gogol, I did not want to tell you on the phone. Ah ... I have decided to sell the house. I am going to do what your father and I had always planned: six months in India and six months here with all of you. Then I can go and start my singing again in Calcutta. That is, if any guru wants a 45-year-old student. [...] I want to be free.

Here, she does not tell them that she is leaving to make herself happy, but merely realizing the plans she and her husband made together. On the surface, she thus remains within fixed structures and the time that she will spend in the U.S. will be devoted to her family. When she ends her announcement by stating that she wants to be free, Moushumi nods: "like your name" and explains "Ashima means 'without borders, limitless.'" Traveling back and forth thus assumes the quality of something predestined, something to be fulfilled by her. Traveling, of course, is also contained in the idea of "following" one's bliss. The fact that she mentions her singing, though, alludes to her desire to respond to her own needs, yet it is naturally also a significant part of Indian tradition. Since it is the only thing that she mentions in the context of her plans in India, it appears to be of major importance to her. I have asserted earlier that singing was a significant part of her identity and offered her a voice. By returning to a life as a student, she will continue to form this voice.

A New Family

Whereas travel ranks especially high in *Mississippi Masala* and *The Namesake*, *Chutney Popcorn* contains another significant theme, namely the building of a new family system. Arora holds that the film ends with a "quasi-utopian vision" of a multicultural family that has been created from the various complicated relationships (32) I have analyzed above. This new family is denaturalized and non-heteronormative, thereby disrupting the importance of biological reproduction and heterosexual lineage that tradition has valued (ibid. 37). In this vein, fathers are absent in the film and while the viewer never learns why Sarita's and Reena's father is not present, Mitch, too, is, to borrow Arora's words, "side-lined" during the conception and the birth of his baby (38).

This is also emphasized in the scene in which Meenu performs a ceremony blessing the unborn child. While Reena is still sleeping, Meenu's loud knocks on the door can be heard. From the end of the corridor, the camera films Lisa opening the door and Meenu entering quickly. "The eighth month is beginning, it's time to do the ceremony," she states and pushes Lisa in front of her down the corridor. Behind her, Mitch and Sarita enter the apartment. The long shot that shows the entire corridor is significant in so far as the viewer realizes that the apartment now differs greatly from the beginning of the film. Now only Reena and Lisa seem to live there, Lisa's boxes that have been standing around everywhere have been cleared out and the whole apartment looks neat and tidy compared to the chaotic setting in which clothes, Reena's photos, boxes of food and other items had been lying around everywhere. The neat apartment also signifies that Reena and Lisa have settled together: Lisa is not ready to pack her things quickly and leave her anymore. Furthermore, they have created a space for their small family. However, apparently it is a space in which their lesbian friends do not have (a) room.

Meenu, on the other hand, has entered the women's apartment for the first time. Arora suggests that while Reena's mother now starts to accept her daughter's choices, the alienation from her lesbian friends is an aspect that deserves consideration. The film depicts the limitations of a "genuinely diasporized queerness" since Reena's white lesbian friends and her family do not understand her desire to fully belong and her identity as both Indian and lesbian (40). After all, the young women were very critical of the pregnancy when they argued that Reena was "being used to perpetuate the heterosexual family model," collapsing Reena's active choice into passive fate and adherence to others' norms. Especially Lisa feared that her girlfriend would lapse into "compulsory heterosexuality" and enter a relationship with Mitch, a fear that leads Arora to the assertion that "[t]hey seem to perceive homosexuality as a poor copy of heterosexuality always in danger of reverting to the superior original" (ibid.).

The beginning of the scene is accompanied by the same music (the "Chutney Popcorn" score produced for the film) as the scene in the beginning, when Reena and Lisa were on their way to Sarita's and Mitch's wedding, which suggests certain parallels. Like the wedding, the ceremony that follows helps to form and then acknowledges the new family unit. Now Sarita has a gift for her sister: a pair of jeans that will now fit her. The gift represents the growing bond between the sisters, since Sarita, unlike her mother, accepts that her sister likes to wear jeans. As she takes them out of the bag and Reena looks at them, the music fades, leading the viewer into the ceremony in which the only sounds come from Meenu's words and movements.

The ceremony takes place in the couple's living room. In the left corner of the frame, a part of their sofa is still visible and on the wall behind them there is a shelf with CDs (see figure 13). Next to it, there are two pieces of Indian art on the wall demonstrating that Indian tradition is part of their lives as well. The center of the frame is occupied by a small table, covered with a red cloth with Indian ornaments, and two chairs that face the camera. Two other chairs have been moved to the side and stand in front of the wall to their right and left. This setting illustrates that Indian tradition and the women's everyday life correlate. They have made room for the ceremony, but it remains incorporated into the everyday and within the structures of their lives.

Moreover, the ritual also establishes the structure of the new family unit, since before she can speak her blessings, Meenu has to decide on positions for everyone: "Reena, you sit here" she orders her daughter to sit on the right chair. Reena immediately covers her head with a scarf. Unlike during a ceremony at the beginning of the film when Meenu blessed the newly-weds' house, she seems to know exactly what to do, a sign that she is now also comfortable in her role as an Indian woman. Sarita is supposed to stand behind her: "You take this umbrella ... Now, open it. Hold it over her." "You are like the brother," Meenu tells her, interestingly assigning a male role to Sarita in the ceremony. Considering that males are absent in the family, Meenu's utterance elucidates that she still feels the need to term the position in the ritual that usually requires a male, as "male." Also the rest of the ceremony will show that Meenu is to some extent flexible in the performance of the ritual, but is careful to observe the established structures. By ordering "you promise to protect your sister," she also strengthens the bond between the sisters and acknowledges that their relationship is just as good as one between brother and sister, thereby undermining the higher status of men in Indian society.

When Sarita opens the umbrella, she almost accidentally hits her mother with it. This shot, among others, underlines the make-shift quality of the ritual – not in the sense that it becomes insincere (although the umbrella does add a humorous dimension), but in the sense that it simply cannot be performed in the traditional way and Meenu needs to be content with what the new setting offers. While Meenu tells her daughters what to do, Lisa and Mitch are standing on the left, Mitch has his hand in his pockets and Lisa has folded her arms. Although they are looking curiously at the sisters and their mother, their gestures emphasize that they are unsure how to react and distance themselves from the ritual, as they do not share blood ties with the family. "This is a ceremony, I've done this twice, on both of them," Meenu says to no one in particular, but probably directed at Mitch and Lisa in order to re-assure them of her cultural authority in light of the make-shift arrangement. Then she moves on to find a suitable place for Lisa. "You ... you're the ... like the husband," she says and sits Lisa down next to Sarita (see figure 13).

She starts her sentence three times until she has found the right utterance, which shows that she still has trouble finding a suitable role for Lisa in her daughter's life. However, by giving her the role of the husband in the ritual, she finally acknowledges their lesbian relationship. Like Sarita's, Lisa's role is appropriated, hence the use of the simile. It seems important

Figure 13: Chutney Popcorn, *finding a place for Lisa in the ceremony*

for Meenu to orient herself around the heteronormative roles that would usually have their place in the ritual.

Finally, she needs to find a place for Mitch, the only male in the family. "And, ah, Mitch ..." she hesitates. This is the only shot in the ritual that constitutes a point-of-view shot from Mitch's perspective, looking at his mother-in-law and thereby actively demanding a place. However, she does not explain a position to him, but silently gestures him to just stand there next to Sarita. The fact that he is the only one that does not take up a role necessary to perform the ceremony illustrates that he is indeed side-lined, as Arora has argued: "Far from being the ultimate figure of authority, the only white heterosexual male in this picture is displaced and relegated to the periphery" (39). In the next step, Reena is asked to open the scarf. "I will put these almonds in your lap, they are a symbol of ... eh, fertility," her mother declares, waves aside and dumps the entire bag of almonds into the scarf, making clear that all of a sudden it does not matter to her anymore whether the ceremony is carried out as prescribed, but she seems to now feel comfortable with fashioning her own ritual.

Just as the family's arrival at the couple's apartment suggested parallels to Lisa's and Reena's arrival the wedding, the aesthetics of the ceremony, too, draw parallels between these two scenes. Throughout the ceremony, Reena and Lisa look at each other several times, smiling. While the camera has remained static up to this point and, through the use of long shots, at a considerable distance from the events, it now focuses on the lesbian lovers in a medium close-up that is reminiscent of the framing of the wedding scene, since the composition of the shot resembles the shot in which Sarita and her husband were sitting in front of their guests. Here the faces of the persons behind them are similarly cut off by the frame so that the women are at the center and their gazes underline their love for each other. Additionally, especially through the parallel to the wedding, the film "exposes and interrupts the frequent employment of family both metonymically and metaphorically to describe and constitute the naturalized, racialized, heteronormative, and gendered relationships between identity and place" (Desai 76).

Nevertheless the newly fashioned family is not accepted without hesitation. "Now, everybody. What to do, oh God?" Another point-of-view shot from the young people toward Meenu shows that she is confused when she looks at the arrangement that she has created. Of course she cannot yet accept the 'unnatural' unity. Nevertheless she goes on to apply the tilaka, a Hindu mark, to all of their foreheads and then to the image of an Indian goddess that stands on the table. Just when she touches the image, the first chords of another rock song ("Slowly, Slowly" by Magnapop) with female vocals emerge. Earlier I have spoken of a "push and pull," to use Arora's words, between the two cultures that was symbolized by the superimposition of rock music on Indian music. Here, this is not the case, since the song does not cut into ongoing music, but only sets in when the ritual seems finished. The Indian and lesbian elements of Reena's identity hence no longer clash and compete against each other. In the context of the queer diasporic/diasporized queer rituals are altered or re-made to provide for a re-imagination of notions of home, identity, family/kinship, community and belonging (Arora 31).

Utopia or Happy Ending?

In the previous chapters and the sections of this chapter I have shown who the protagonists are, what kind of conflicts they face and how they have successfully solved these conflicts by the end of each plot. In this last section I will now examine the final shots of each film to assess their happy endings. Perhaps notions of "self-fulfillment" or "agency," might have worked equally well in the title of this section as they stress their importance for each of the female protagonists. Despite the fact that these issues are of great significance to the understanding of the endings, they are only the first step in an analysis and in the context of transnational cinema a possible reading of the endings has to go beyond that.

The endings of the films make clear that there is no formulaic happy ending for transnational films. Their attempts to provide a happy outcome are as multifaceted as their genres, protagonists, and their individual situations, yet the readings so far have shown that the films do indeed strongly adhere to genre specific conventions and their happy ending plays a crucial role in this. A notion that much of the criticism on the films hence employs with respect to their happy endings is that of 'utopia.' Frequently encountered in literary works of art, utopias address a collective problem and aim to be transformative (Levitas 188). Since they are often consulted in times of cultural and societal crises, utopian visions are essentially a modern phenomenon (Schwendter 21f., Levitas ibid.). Literally a "not-place," utopia often signifies a place located away from the present society (Schwendter 19). According to social scientist Rolf Schwendter, utopia is the negation of an ill situation in the present (21f). However, sociologist Ruth Levitas stresses that utopias are neither intended to constitute political programs nor present convincing agendas for change, but rather express desire (188). They may be critical of the status quo, but ultimately Levitas does not attribute utopias with the capacity to effectively challenge the present situation (196, 188). Although 'utopia' is all too often used in an unreflected manner as a synonym for something plainly unrealistic, the endings of the films do indeed reflect the desire and social critique associated with utopian visions. Accordingly, this section aims to clarify what kind of desire the films express in their final shots and in how far the endings of the films criticize the status quo.

First of all, each of the films employs flash-forwards in the final scenes to take the viewers to an undefined point in future time. *Mississippi Masala* leaves viewers with a sequence of shots that portray Demetrius and Mina in traditional African and Indian garments in front of a wide open space. *Chutney Popcorn* closes with a series of photographs that depict the Reena with her friends, family, and the baby and *The Namesake* ends with Ashima sitting outside taking singing lessons. In light of these endings, several questions arise, such as "Why does Demetrius wear traditional clothes when he has never paid attention to tradition?" or "When did Becca and Janis make up with Reena?" In the final shots, these questions remain of course unanswered and viewers are at first overwhelmed by the harmonious impressions that end the films. In contrast to utopia as defined above, though, the visions which the films offer are not located away from society or in secret locales, but are firmly localized, in case of *Mississippi Masala* and *Chutney Popcorn* in the U.S. and in *The Namesake* in India. Therefore the vision receives a concrete setting.

The two plotlines of *Mississippi Masala* – Jay's brief return to Uganda and Mina's and Demetrius's departure – both end in images of harmony. After he has decided to leave Uganda, Jay is drawn towards a crowd of Blacks watching a dancer. They step aside and allow Jay to join their circle. Moreover, a Black child touches him, a touch that reminds one of Jay's memory of his friendship to Okelo. For a moment the child connects Jay and the Black father who both turn their smiles and gazes towards the child. Then Jay accepts, takes the child into a tight embrace. The scene suggests the possibility of reconciliation and provides a sense of closure, ending Jay's racism. Moreover, the Black child may foreshadow a future between Mina and Demetrius. The diegetic music in this scene is a song by a Ugandan group that conveys joy and happiness, underlined by the Black woman dancing in the center of the crowd. This song continues after the last shot of the Ugandan setting has faded and the closing credits start. These credits are interrupted by three brief scenes which, through the song, are connected to Jay's experience in Uganda.

All three scenes depict Demetrius and Mina at the side of a road. It is not clear how much time has passed, yet both of them now wear traditional clothes. In the first scene, the road appears as a straight horizontal line with cotton fields on both sides and behind the road, the fields are stretched out to the horizon, emphasizing the vast open range. Half of the frame is occupied by a blue and almost clear sky, another element that underlines the openness of the setting. Demetrius is holding Mina in his arms and spins her through the air as he walks further into the field. Their jolly moves remind the viewer of their ride on the whirlygig in Biloxi, where they decided to travel to any place they liked.

The second scene takes place in the same setting, yet now the two are standing close to each other and kiss (see figure 14). As the camera cir-

Figure 14: Mississippi Masala, *ending*

cles around them, the van becomes visible – apparently still their vehicle on their journey – as well as the vast open range everywhere around them. The dynamic of the first scene is sustained by the moving camera, so that this scene, too, depicts movement. Finally, the third scene begins with a close-up of Mina's and Demetrius's hands at the side of their bodies. The camera follows when Demetrius's hand takes Mina's, and the last shot then shows them with their eyes closed, kissing. Whereas the camera has gradually approached the lovers during the last two scenes, it now views them from a fixed perspective and a slightly lower angle, as to show the lovers' sublimity.

Several critics assert that toward the end of *Mississippi Masala*, Mina becomes American (Girgus 29). Desai adds that this is realized by Mina's coming of age in the "standard American narrative of becoming sexually active" (86). As a consequence, Mina separates from her oppressive Indian community to complete the rites of passage that make her American (ibid.). My analysis so far has shown that a clear-cut distinction between American, Indian, and Ugandan cannot grasp Mina's self-fashioned identity, since why else would she introduce herself in a flirt with Demetrius as a 'masala,' "a mixture of hot spices"? Furthermore, both Mina and Demetrius wear traditional outfits, Mina an Indian dress and Demetrius African clothes. This is striking considering that Demetrius has never valued tradition highly or even mentioned a connection to Africa. It is an illogical step in the plot that idealizes the image of the lovers and produces a utopian final picture. At the same time, it serves to balance the influence of America on them, so that Kaplan's critique that the film puts American values of freedom and individual choice before those of traditional culture is not valid anymore (177). Unlike Desai, who believes that sexual activity "mobilizes and nationalizes migrant women" (86), I want to emphasize that her mobility also stems from her idea to run a business with Demetrius.

Similarly, Girgus considers the couple as icons for a middle-class America that values individuality, self-discipline and work (31). To create something out of nearly nothing except dedication, energy and will to him represents the renewal of a core American idea, embodied in people of color: "Nair's film reexamines American cultural and national history to articulate, problematize and complicate the myth and ideology of America as a New World Garden inhabited by all peoples of the world who cohere together to form a distinctly new race" (38, 22). Still, despite all the positive connotations that the ending carries, I take a critical view of the fact that Mina can only leave with Demetrius and not alone, for it compromises her agency to some extent, making her journey dependent on a man.

In the last section I have suggested that *Chutney Popcorn* ends with a "quasi-utopian vision" of a new family (Arora 32). Like *Mississippi Masala*, the last scenes of the film consist of recorded moments, this time in photographs that have no clear relation to place and time. Various black and white images show the family and the new baby outside. The sequence consists of a close-up of the baby, photos of Meenu, Mitch and Reena each holding her, Sarita holding her, while Reena and Meenu are sitting across from her, one of the lesbian friends with the baby, another one holding a white baby-size t-shirt on which "Girls kick ass!" has been written, two photos of Reena and Lisa with the child, and finally one with the entire family. All these photos constitute recordings of happy moments, with the sitters smiling. Furthermore, they all seem to have been taken on the same day, since the people are wearing the same clothes in each photograph. The setting, too, seems to be the same in most pictures; as streets, houses and cars can be recognized in the background, they have probably been taken in the urban area in which Reena and Lisa are at home.

Pisters and Staat argue that although the normative definition of a family traditionally consists of (white) heterosexual parents and their children, this definition can be extended "as long as it is considered as a group of people that care for each other and provide children a safe place to grow up" (8). The photos present a further step in the rapprochement of Reena's two families, her Indian and her chosen lesbian. Since her mother has already accepted Lisa, she is of course featured in a number of the shots. On top of that, also Becca and Janis, the two young women who used to live with Lisa and Reena, are shown in the photos. The plot leaves the viewer with a gap here, since the last encounter between the lesbian women depicted them as highly critical of Reena's plan and it seemed that, in order to become a part of one family, Reena had to accept alienation from the other. It is precisely this idea of the gap, the tenuous plot, which critics such as Arora praise:

> Reena's two families have started to come together, not necessarily *sans* friction, and the emerging kinship network is one based on love, support, durability and loyalty. The potential of the film's ending lies in its tenuousness, in its presentation of the possibility of a re-figured family unit that extends the notion of family, not limited to the idea of a biological one, a queer family or an ethnic community. (40)

The final shot of the film, however, disrupts this impression and also counters Arora's argument. In the last photo, Meenu and the child occupy the center, Mitch and Sarita sit on the right, Reena on the left, while Lisa is kneeling in the back, between Meenu and Mitch (see figure 15). Despite the fact that all the sitters are smiling in the photo, this final image leaves viewers with an ambiguous impression and compromises the new family unit the film has worked to construct, for in the photo it becomes obvious that not Reena, Lisa, and their relationship are at the center anymore but it is indeed the close connection between Sarita, Mitch, Meenu, and the baby

Figure 15: Chutney Popcorn, *last shot*

the photo elucidates. Sitting close to each other, legs and hands entangled, Sarita and Meenu face each other and their body postures provide a frame for the baby and also for Mitch, who, although occupying a position behind his wife and mother-in-law, is part of the unity. Lisa and especially Reena, however, are excluded and lean into the half-circle the other three have formed and in which their backs face them. Both women hold on to Meenu, yet Reena's posture in particular illustrates that there is distance between her and her mother, symbolized through the space gap between the two bodies. As a result, this final shot not only directs attention away from the lesbian relationship and reverts back to a privileging of the traditional family structure, but also revealingly relocates both Meenu and Mitch in center positions. The still thus confirms the importance of Meenu as an authority in the characters' lives, and, perhaps more problematic, for the first time in the entire film assigns a central role to the white heterosexual Mitch in this familial unity.

It is due to the final shot, but also on account of the entire closing sequence that Arora's celebration of the film is not fully warrantable. The ending of the film shows that the plot remains tied to the conventions of Hollywood cinema, for the narrative ends with impressions of a happy reunion and does not move on to show the everyday life of this new family (Arora 40). Unlike the other two films, *Chutney Popcorn* ends its plot with photographic snapshots. Of course they are an allusion to Reena's passion for photography and represent moments that have been recorded to be remembered, maybe put on display. Yet undoubtedly, the new support system depicted here may present a threat to the traditional nuclear family, which is one reason why their trip to the park is not presented in actual colored shots, but only preserved in photo stills that allow for greater distance.

The last scene of *The Namesake* depicts Ashima back in Calcutta, one of the two locales of her ongoing travels. Outside, she is sitting on a small platform on white cushions, with her teacher is sitting next to her, while other, younger, students sit on the ground. Ashima is completely absorbed in the music – this time, she accompanies herself on the instrument – and her singing, her eyes fixed on the teacher only for a moment, then half-closed to concentrate fully on the music and herself. The teacher assumes the role of the conductor, visibly shakes his head and gestures disagreement. The camera, though, slowly zooms in on Ashima, hence simply fading out the teacher who certainly criticizes or corrects her. For the time being, what matters are Ashima and her song. Nonetheless, I do not read this scene in the sense that Ashima, using her own voice, completely turns away from instruction. In this case, the teacher would no longer be necessary. Secondly, when she ends her song, she looks into the direction of her teacher and smiles in an expression of deep happiness (cf. figure 16).

All in all, the films carefully mediate the crises they have introduced. Consistent with the feminist dictum "the personal is political," the films tell personal stories in exposure to the cultural crisis that transnationalism presents: *Mississippi Masala* proposes the continuous journey as a resolution to Mina's double displacement, *Chutney Popcorn* delineates an alternative to the traditional family in order to allow Reena to fashion an identity in which her Indianness and homosexuality may merge, and *The Namesake*, too, suggests that traveling presents a viable alternative to Ashima's dis-

Figure 16: The Namesake, *Ashima in India*

placement in the U.S. and her desire to connect with her children and their bicultural families in the United States. Each of these story therefore contributes to a bigger picture of the mediation of displacement through both expulsion and immigration. However, these crises are mediated against the background of American life on the one hand and traditional Indian life on the other. Although choice is a major factor in the decision-making process of the protagonists, it is concealed behind either American values or Indian tradition. Ultimately, the protagonists remain to a certain extent confined, while at the same time, the films show how strong the influence of the national within the transnational context still is.

By carefully balancing aspects such as tradition and the individual pursuit of happiness, the films do indeed pick up the issue of resistance and reconciliation which I mentioned at the beginning of this chapter. On the level of both content and aesthetics, they resist tradition and heteronormativity, as well as certain genre-specific expectations, but eventually offer reconciliation by either revoking some of the more dramatic instances of resistance, as in the case of *Chutney Popcorn*, or by putting genre conventions and traditional values to work, like in *Mississippi Masala* and *The Namesake*. At the same time they show that an alternative vision, a utopian ending if you will, cannot remain detached from cultural values, but has to rework them, much in the sense of Jahn-Sudmann's reminder that in transnationalism "borders are not overcome in a way that is lasting, but it is the prospect of overcoming that matters" (26).

Conclusion

The films under analysis here, as well as numerous other productions, portray transnationalism as a cultural crisis in which ethnic communities and families begin to disintegrate in the course of forced or voluntary migration and the ensuing contact with the American value system. The transnational world with its subjects on the move is not one in which the characters may use their connections beyond the respective nation-states to full potential, but one in which many of the characters – at least initially – yearn for stability and their homeland, feel alienated and excluded. It is their coming to terms with the transnational condition the films render for their, equally transnational, audiences. In this vein, I have argued that transnational cinema becomes an instrument in the mediation of the cultural crises the changes of a transnational world present.

These crises are powerfully elucidated at the beginnings of the films when protagonists who are both displaced from their homelands and "out of place" in their respective communities cause a stir and set into motion numerous, seemingly insurmountable conflicts: In *Mississippi Masala*, Mina is highly dissatisfied with her position between the two poles of American and Indian culture, unable and unwilling to fully participate in either community. Moreover, once her secret relationship to the Black Demetrius is exposed, the film sheds light on the fact that the multicultural Greenwood community is deeply divided on grounds of racial prejudices and likewise, racism is a significant issue in Jay's relation to the family's homeland in Africa. In Ganatra's *Chutney Popcorn*, the issue of "being out of place" is intensified through the fact that the protagonist Reena is a lesbian and lesbianism and Indianness continue to clash throughout the film as Reena's mother refuses to acknowledge her sexuality. Yet whereas the protagonists of these two films are already in the U.S., *The Namesake* introduces Ashima as a young classical singer in India who not only immerses herself in Indian traditional practices, but is also fully integrated into her community there. Moving to the U.S. after she has married Ashoke entails psychological consequences that are not remediated until the end of film. Transnational themes, such as expulsion, migration, alienation, and the push and pull within multinational and multicultural communities therefore propel the films' plots and the protagonists' newly-formed relationships carry great weight in these crises.

However, instead of resisting and turning away from genre-specific conventions, as Strobel has asserted (9), transnational cinema well employs aspects of Hollywood genres, which at times, my analysis has shown, are reinforced, first of all by the fact that all three films end happily given the momentousness of the crises their characters have initially faced. Secondly, all films convey a message that favors romantic love. Both *Mississippi Masala* and *Chutney Popcorn* move back and forth between different couples, illustrating that neither arranged marriage nor the fulfillment of cultural expectations brings about happiness and the protagonists' love prevails against all odds. In *The Namesake*, arranged marriage is problematized in the initial scenes depicting the newly-weds in their American home, yet in their relationship, too, love eventually triumphs over emotional distance, a plot development catering to Western audiences. Third, the close reading of *Mississippi Masala* in particular illustrates that the film strongly adheres to the conventions of the romantic comedy. On the one hand, one may of course argue that the formulaic plot of this transnational film effectively undermines the white 'normalcy' which has long dominated the Hollywood screen, for Nair's film fills the Western form with the voices and stories of ethnic characters while at the same time relegating white American characters in unappealing and marginal roles. On the other hand, this also raises the question whether Mina's and Demetrius's story cannot be told in other terms than the popular – and commercially successful – Western script. The films certainly bespeak the prominence and significance of Hollywood and its genres and simultaneously presuppose a Western audience whose expectations the films are careful to fulfill.

Nonetheless, the films also contain significant disruptive moments which subvert established genre conventions and use these disruptions to explore the transnational condition. In contrast to the Hollywood romantic comedy, the films' plots do not follow the conventional marriage plot. While weddings scenes of course serve to establish new family structures in all films, in *Mississippi Masala* and *Chutney Popcorn* these scenes also provide the character constellation with a couple in stark contrast to the protagonists and their love relationships. The institution of marriage is then either denaturalized (*Chutney Popcorn*) or mocked on account of the spouses' adherence to Indian traditions (*Mississippi Masala*). Marriage, intricately linked to (the illusion of) permanence and stability, does therefore not resonate with the characters in the transnational setting.

A second disruptive moment becomes evident when the films, and *The Namesake* is a particularly revealing example here, first of all challenge assimilation in undermining the notion that suburbanization presents assimilation and then moving on to turn the suburban dream into a nightmare when the family's home in the suburbs becomes the site for traumatic encounters and thus needs to be abandoned. In the other films, the non-place becomes a preferred setting and constitutes a significant site of identity formation processes in transnational fashion, which leads to the third disruptive moment in the films. The filmic visions of the transnational are no longer concerned with showing an arrival in certain destinations, possibly a return to the protagonists' home country, but instead end in departures, often avoiding full closure. Travel becomes a meaningful aspect since subjects with a "nonchalant detachment" from their home can continue to form their identity (Braidotti, *Nomadic* 20). Hence the narratives end with their protagonists being on the road or in the midst of a new journey: Mina and Demetrius leave Greenwood, Sarita rides the motorcycle, and Ashima will continue to travel between India and the United States.

Moreover, the narratives discussed here carefully balance American exceptionalism and ethnic traditions, so that the idea of resistance and reconciliation is indeed appropriate here and does not only hold true for the characters' relationships but in equal measure also for their connections with their respective ethnic communities. Nonetheless one should not neglect the fact that by concealing the protagonists' choices behind either American or Indian values, the protagonists remain to some extent confined. Finally, the films hence show how strong the power of nationalisms within the transnational still is and elucidate a lasting problem in transnational theory.

In this vein, scholarship on transnational cinema needs to continue probing the interrelations between the national and the transnational, between the local and the global, and examine what may even present itself as a master narrative in transnational discourse, namely the strong influence of the national, both on the level of content and when it comes to the films' modes of production. With film scholars Will Higbee and Song Hwee Lim, I urge critics not to simply cast aside and negate the concept of the 'national' in the analysis of internationally produced films (10). On the plane of form, scholars may further investigate the issue of formalistic 'translations,' as this book has begun to do, and study the application of aesthetics and a specific filmic language to stories in an international context to not only clarify to what extent and to which ends the stories of the diaspora borrow from Hollywood conventions, but to also illustrate how commercially successful Western cinema employs the conventions of other 'national' cinemas. Quentin Tarantino's *Kill Bill*, for example, lends itself to a reading with regard to the translation of the filmic language usually employed in the *kung fu* cinema of Hong Kong, as critics have demonstrated. How may such translations transform a cinema like Hollywood in the long run?

Furthermore, scholars of transnational film may engage in discussions of 'thematic translations,' as media and cultural studies scholar Jeroen de Kloet has done in his essay on Taiwanese director Ang Lee's oeuvre and his thematic translation of the Chinese family into different places and periods of time which produces new meanings that in the "original" have been rendered either invisible or unspeakable (120f.). Similarly, we might trace the ways in which "translations" travel from the U.S. around the globe or examine texts that "translate" originals into an American context to pose the question of how these thematic translations work to critique national "originals." Without doubt, the study of these flows of intertextuality will take scholarly endeavors not only beyond national borders, spurring discussions of the United States and its embeddedness into international contexts, but also beyond the established boundaries of disciplines (Davis 6).

Finally, scholarship on transnational cinema also needs to investigate the relationship between the transnational and the national off-screen. With regard to the films' production contexts, attention might not only be devoted to the question of which international co-productions and collaborations bring forth transnational films and what such collaborations imply on an aesthetic, political, and economic level (Higbee and Lee 10), but also from where the capital necessary to realize these productions flows and where the respective productions receive particular recognition. Again, we might ask for the economic, political, and aesthetic implications of these observations and use them to scrutinize the 'transnational' in transnational cinema. Similarly, we might study audiences and their places and means of consuming transnational cinema. In how far do the internet and video-on-demand or streaming-services impact audiences and can they help to transcend the binary of the transnational and the national?

In the context of American Studies, such critical engagement with transnational cinema will enable us, Rocío Davis hopes, to "formulate or envision connections between the United States and the world" and bring "new maturity" into the discourses of American Studies (5, 10). It might not render borders permanently invisible or meaningless, but it will certainly demonstrate and help to appreciate the fluidity and permeability of borders in today's transnational world.

WORKS CITED AND FURTHER RESOURCES

Adeeko, Adeleke. "*Mississippi Masala*: Crossing Desire and Interest." in: *Reversing the Lens: Ethnicity. Race, Gender, and Sexuality through Film.* Eds. Jun Xing and Lane Ryo Hirabayashi. Boulder: UP of Colorado, 2003. 127–42. Print.

Arora, Anupama. "Rituals of Queer Diaspora in Nisha Ganatra's *Chutney Popcorn*." *South Asian Popular Culture*. 5.1 (2007): 31–43. Print.

Ashcroft, Bill. "The Emperor's New Clothes: Global (Dis)Affections." in: *Postcolonial (Dis)Affections*. Eds. Walter Göbel and Saskia Schabio. Trier: Wissenschaftlicher Verlag Trier, 2007. 9–23. Print.

Augé, Marc. *Non-Places: Introduction to an Anthropology of Supermodernity*. London: Verso, 1995. Print.

Ba, Saer Maty and Will Higbee. "Re-presenting Aiasporas in Cinema and New (Digital) Media: Introduction." *Journal of Media Practice* 11.1 (2010): 3–10. Print.

Bahri Deepika and Mary Vasudeva (eds.). *Between the Lines: South Asians and Postcoloniality*. Philapelhia: Temple UP, 1996. Print.

Berger, Bennett M. "Suburbia and the American Dream." *National Affairs* 2 (1966): 80–96. Print.

Bhabha, Homi. *Location of Culture*. London: Routledge, 1994. Print.

Bidney, David. "The Concept of Cultural Crisis." *American Anthropologist New Series* 48.4 (1946): 534–52. Print.

Binici, Ozhan. "Portraits from Non-Places." *Transmission*. 2008. Web. 4 Aug. 2014.

Bourne, Randolph. "Trans-National America." *Atlantic Monthly* 118 (1916): 86–97. Web. 4 Aug. 2014.

Braidotti, Rosi. *Nomadic Subjects: Embodiment and Sexual Difference in Cotemporary Feminist Theory*. New York: Columbia UP, 1994. Print.

—. "Nomadism with a Difference: Deleuze's Legacy in a Feminist Perspective." *Man and World* 29 (1996): 305–14. Print.

Buscombe, Edward. "The Idea of Genre in American Cinema." in: *Film Genre Reader II*. Ed. Barry Keith Grant. Austin: U of Texas P, 1995. 11–25. Print.

Chen, Tina Mai and David S. Churchill (eds.). *Film, History, and Cultural Citizenship: Sites of Production*. London/New York: Routledge, 2007. Print.

Cheung, Ruby and D. H. Fleming (eds.). *Cinemas, Identities and Beyond*. Newcastle: Cambridge Scholars, 2009. Print.

Chutney Popcorn. Dir. Nisha Ganatra. Homescreen. 1991. DVD.

Collins, Patricia Hill. "It's all in the Family: Intersections of Gender, Race, and Nation." in: *Decentering the Center: Philosophy for a Multicultural, Postcolonial and Feminist World*. Eds. Uma Narayan and Sandra Harding. Bloomington: Indiana UP, 2000. 156–76. Print.

Cook, Pam (eds.). *The Cinema Book*. London: BFI, 2007. Print.

Corrigan, Timothy and Patricia Hill. *The Film Experience: An Introduction*. 3rd Ed. Boston/New York: Bedford/St. Martin's, 2004. Print.

Coyne, Richard. "Orienting the Future: Design Strategies for Non-Place." *Designing for the 21st Century*. n.d. Web. 4 Aug. 2014.

Dayal, Samir. "Diaspora and Double Consciousness." *The Journal of the Midwest Modern Language Association*. 29.1 (1996): 46–62. Print.

Davis, Rocío G. "Introduction." in: *The Transnationalism of American Culture*. Ed. Rocío G. Davis. New York: Routledge, 2013. 1–13. Print.

de Kloet, Jeroen. "Saved by Betrayal? Ang Lee's Translations of 'Chinese' Family Ideology." in: *Shooting the Family. Transnational Media and Intercultural Values*. Eds. Patricia Pisters and Wim Staat. Amsterdam: Amsterdam UP, 2005. 117–32. Print.

de Leeuw, Sonja. "Migrant Children Mediating Family Relations." in: *Shooting the Family. Transnational Media and Intercultural Values*. Eds. Patricia Pisters and Wim Staat. Amsterdam: Amsterdam UP, 2005. 41–55. Print.

Desai, Jigna. *Beyond Bollywood: The Cultural Politics of South Asian Diasporic Film*. London: Routledge, 2004. Print.

Dolby, Sandra K. *Self-Help Books. Why Americans Keep Reading Them*. Chicago: U of Illinois P, 2005. Print.

Dowd, James J. and Nicole R. Pallotta. "The End of Romance: The Demystification of Love in the Postmodern Age." *Sociological Perspectives* 43.4 (2000): 549–80. Print.

"Drama." *Allmovie.com.* 2010. Web. 14 July 2010.

Elliott, Emory. "Diversity in the United States and Abroad: What Does it Mean when American Studies is Transnational?" *American Quarterly* 59.1 (2007): 1–22. Print.

Ezra, Elizabeth and Terry Rowden. "General Introduction: What is Transnational Cinema?" in: *Transnational Cinema: The Film Reader.* Eds. Elizabeth Ezra and Terry Rowden. London: Routledge, 2006. 1–12. Print.

Featherstone, Simon. *Postcolonial Cultures.* Edinburgh: Edinburgh UP, 2005. Print.

Feng, Peter (eds.). *Screening Asian Americans.* New Brunswick: Rutgers UP, 2002. Print.

—. *Identities in Motion: Asian American Film and Video.* Durham/London: Duke, 2003. Print.

Fisher Fishkin, Shelley. "Crossroads of Cultures: The Transnational Turn in American Studies – Presidential Address to the American Studies Association, November 12, 2004." *American Quarterly* 57.1 (2005): 17–57. Print.

—. "Mapping American Studies in the Twenty-First Century: Transnational Perspectives." in: *The Transnationalism of American Culture.* Ed. Rocío G. Davis. New York: Routledge, 2013. 14–30. Print.

Fluck, Winfried. "Theories of American Culture (and the Transnational Turn in American Studies." in: *Transnational American Studies.* Eds. Winfried Fluck, Stefan Brandt and Ingrid Thaler. Tübingen: Narr, 2007. 59–78. Print.

Fluck, Winfried, Stefan Brandt and Ingrid Thaler. "Introduction: The Challenges of Transnational American Studies." in: *Transnational American Studies.* Eds. Winfried Fluck, Stefan Brandt and Ingrid Thaler. Tübingen: Narr, 2007. 1–7. Print.

Friedman, Natalie. "From Hybrids to Tourists: Children of Immigrants in Jhumpa Lahiri's *The Namesake.*" *Critique: Studies in Contemporary Fiction* 50.1 (2008): 111–28. Print.

Girgus, Sam. *America on Film. Modernism, Documentary and a Changing America.* Cambridge: Cambridge UP, 2002. Print.

Glick Schiller, Nina, Linda Basch and Cristina Blanc-Szanton. "Towards a Definition of Transnationalism: Introductory Remarks and Research Questions." in: *Towards a Transnational Perspective on Migration: Race, Class, Ethnicity and Nationalism Reconsidered.* Eds. Nina Glick Schiller, Linda Basch and Cristina Blanc-Szanton. New York: New York Academy of Sciences, 1992. ix-xiv. Print.

Gopinath, Gayatri. *Impossible Desires: Queer Diasporas and South Asian Public Cultures.* Durham: Duke UP, 2005. Print.

Grassilli, Mariagiulia. "Migrant Cinema: Transnational and Guerrilla Practices of Film Production and Representation." *Journal of Ethnic and Migration Studies* 34.8 (2008): 1237–55. Print.

Grewal, Inderpal. *Transnational America: Feminisms, Diasporas, Neoliberalisms.* Durham: Duke UP, 2005. Print.

Grice, Helena. *Negotiating Identities: An Introduction to Asian American Women's Writing.* Manchester: Manchester UP, 2002. Print.

Grindon, Leger. *The Hollywood Romantic Comedy.* Oxford: Blackwell Publishing, 2011. Print.

Heffelfinger, Elizabeth and Laura Wright. *Visual Difference: Postcolonial Studies and Intercultural Cinema.* New York: Peter Lang, 2011. Print.

Higbee, Will and Song Hwee Lim. "Concepts of Transnational Cinema: Towards a Critical Transnationalism in Film Studies." *Transnational Cinemas* 1.1 (2010): 7–21. Print.

Higson, Andrew. "The Limiting Imagination of National Cinema." in: *Transnational Cinema: The Film Reader.* Eds. Elizabeth Ezra and Terry Rowden. London: Routledge, 2006. 15–25. Print.

Hjort, Mette and Scott MacKenzie (eds.). *Cinema and Nation.* London/New York: Routledge, 2000. Print.

Holmlund, Chris and Justin Wyatt (eds.). *Contemporary American Independent Film.* London/New York: Routledge, 2005. Print.

hooks, bell. *Reel to Real: Race, Sex and Class at the Movies.* New York: Routledge, 1996. Print.

Jahn-Sudmann, Andreas. "Film und Transnationalität: Forschungsperspektiven." in: *Film Transnational und Transkulturell. Europäische und Amerikanische Perspektiven.* Eds. Ricarda Strobel and Andreas Jahn-Sudmann. München: Fink, 2009. 15–26. Print.

Kaplan, E. Ann. *Looking for the Other: Feminism, Film, and the Imperial Gaze.* London: Routledge, 1997. Print.
Kilbourn, Russel J. A. *Cinema, Memory, Modernity: The Representation of Memory from the Art Film to Transnational Cinema.* New York/London: Routledge, 2010. Print.
Koshy, Susan. "The Fiction of Asian American Literature." *The Yale Journal of Criticism* 9 (1996): 315–46. Print.
Kunow, Rüdiger and Wilfried Raussert. "Cultural Memory and Multiple Identities: An Interdisciplinary Approach to 20th Century Identity Politics." in: *Cultural Memory and Multiple Identities.* Eds. Rüdiger Kunow and Wilfried Raussert. Münster: LIT, 2008. 7–18. Print.
Lahiri, Himadri. "Individual-Family Interface in Jhumpa Lahiri's *The Namesake.*" *Americana: E-Journal of American Studies in Hungary* 4.2 (2008): 1–8. Web.
Levitas, Ruth. *The Concept of Utopia.* Bern: Peter Lang, 2010. Print.
Lien, Pei-Te, Margaret Conway and Janelle Wong. *The Politics of Asian Americans. Diversity and Community.* New York: Routledge, 2004. Print.
Lucy, William H. and David L. Phillis. *Tomorrow's Cities, Tomorrow's Suburbs.* Chicago: The U of Chicago P, 2006. Print.
Ma, Sheng-mei. "Tears of Asian Diaspora in *The Namesake*: Empathetic Nostalgia from an Eyehole." *Diaspora Literature and Visual Culture: Asia in Flight.* London/New York: Routledge, 2011. 112–25. Print.
Manzanas, Ana M. and Jesús Benito Sanchez. *Cities, Borders and Spaces in Intercultural American Literature and Film.* New York/London: Routledge, 2011. Print.
Martiniello Marco and Jean-Michel Lafleur. "Ethnic Minorities' Cultural and Artistic Practices as Forms of Political Expression: A Review of the Literature and a Theoretical Discussion on Music." *Journal of Ethnic and Migration Studies* 34.8 (2008): 1191–215. Print.
Mehta, Binita. "Emigrants Twice Displaced: Race, Color, and Identity in Mira Nair's *Mississippi Masala.*" in: *Multiculturalism, Postcoloniality, and Transnational Media.* Eds. Ella Sohat and Robert Stam. New Brunswick: Rutgers UP, 2003. 153–69. Print.
Mississippi Masala. Dir. Mira Nair. The Samuel Goldwyn Company. 1991. DVD.

Monaco, James. *How to Read a Film: Movies, Media, and Beyond.* 4th Ed. Oxford: Oxford UP, 2009. Print.
Muir, John Kenneth. *Mercy in Her Eyes: The Films of Mira Nair.* New York: Applause Cinema and Theater Books, 2006. Print.
Naficy, Hamid. *Accented Cinema: Exilic and Diasporic Filmmaking.* Princeton: Princeton UP, 2001. Print.
—. "Phobic Spaces and Liminal Panics: Independent Transnational Film Genre." in: *Multiculturalism, Postcoloniality, and Transnational Media.* Eds. Ella Sohat and Robert Stam. New Brunswick: Rutgers UP, 2003. 203–26. Print.
—. "Situating Accented Cinema." in: *Transnational Cinema: The Film Reader.* Eds. Elizabeth Ezra and Terry Rowden. London: Routledge, 2006. 111–30. Print.
Nelmes, Jill. *Introduction to Film Studies.* 5th Ed. London/New York: Routledge, 2012. Print.
Nicolaides Becky M. and Andrew Wiese (eds.). *The Suburb Reader.* New York: Routledge, 2006. Print.
Nielsen, John. "Cul-de-sacs: Suburban Dream or Dead End." *NPR.* 7 June 2006. Web. 4 Aug. 2014.
O'Beirne, Emer. "Mapping the Non-Lieu in Marc Augé's Writings." *Forum for Modern Language Studies* 42.1 (2006): 38–50. Print.
Ostendorf, Berndt. *Transnational America: The Fading Borders of the Western Hemisphere.* Heidelberg: Winter, 2002. Print.
Palmer, Landon. "Culture Warrior: 'Sex' and the Romantic Comedy." *Film School Rejects.* 1 June 2010. Web. 4 Aug. 2014.
Piggly Wiggly. "About Us." 2009. Web. 4 Aug. 2014.
Pisters, Patricia and Wim Staat. "Introduction." in: *Shooting the Family. Transnational Media and Intercultural Values.* Eds. Patricia Pisters and Wim Staat. Amsterdam: Amsterdam UP, 2005. 7–24. Print.
Rodriguez, Gregory. "Suburbia Gains an Accent." *New America Foundation.* 28 Dec. 2003. Web. 4 Aug. 2014.
"Romantic Comedy." *Film Reference.* 2010. Web. 21 July 2010.
Rowe, John Carlos. "Post-Nationalism, Globalism and the New American Studies." in: *Post-Nationalist American Studies.* Ed. John Carlos Rowe. Berkeley: U of California P, 2000. 23–37. Print.

Santas, Constantine. *Responding to Film: A Text Guide for Students of Cinema Art.* Chicago: Burnham, 2002. Print.
Sarkar, Bhaskar. "Postcolonial and Transnational Perspectives." in: *The SAGE Handbook of Film Studies.* Eds. James Donald and Michael Renov. London/Thousand Oaks: SAGE, 2008. 123–144. Print.
Schwendter, Rolf. *Utopie. Überlegungen zu einem Zeitlosen Begriff.* Berlin: Seb, 1994. Print.
Seshagiri, Urmila. "At the Crossroads of Two Empires: Mira Nair's *Mississippi Masala* and the Limits of Hybridity." *JAAS* 6.2 (2003): 177–98. Print.
Singh, Jaspal Kaur. *Representation and Resistance. South Asian and African Women's Texts at Home and in the Diaspora.* Calgary: U of Calgary P, 2008. Print.
Smukler, Maya Montañez. "Race, Suburbia, and the Televised American Dream." 2008. Web. 2 Aug. 2014.
Stanford Friedman, Susan. "Beyond White and Other: Relationality and Narrative of Race in Feminist Discourse." *Signs* 21.1 (1995): 1–49. Print.
Stilz, Gerhard. "Widerstand und Versöhnung. Von der Theorie zur Praxis." in: *Zwischen Kontakt und Konflikt: Perspektiven der Postkolonialismus-Forschung.* Eds. Gisela Febel et al. Trier: Wissenschaftlicher Verlag Trier, 2006. 51–61. Print.
Strobel, Ricarda. "Einleitung." in: *Film Transnational und Transkulturell. Europäische und Amerikanische Perspektiven.* Eds. Ricarda Strobel and Andreas Jahn-Sudmann. München: Fink, 2009. 7–13. Print.
Stuart, Andrea. "Mira Nair: A New Hybrid Cinema." in: *Women and Film: A Sight and Sound Reader.* Eds. Pam Cook and Philip Dodd. Philadelphia: Temple UP, 1993. 210–16. Print.
The Namesake. Dir. Mira Nair. 20th Century Fox. 2006. DVD.
Tudor, Andrew. "Genre." in: *Film Genre Reader II.* Ed. Barry Keith Grant. Austin: U of Texas P, 1995. 3–10. Print.
Vertovec, Steven. *Transnationalism.* London: Routledge, 2009. Print.
Voicu, Christina-Georgiana. "Crossing Borders: Journey into Otherness." Cultural and Linguistic Communication 1.4 (2011): 322–39. Print.
Wartenberg, Thomas E. *Unlikely Couples: Movie Romance as Social Criticism.* Boulder: Westview Press, 1999. Print.

Williams, Allan (ed.). *Film and Nationalism*. New Brunswick/London: Rutgers UP, 2002. Print.

Wong, Sau-Ling C. "Denationalization Reconsidered: Asian American Cultural Criticism at a Theoretical Crossroads." *Amerasia Journal* 21.1–2 (1995): 1–27. Print.